OPENING TO CHINA

Opening to China

A Memoir of Normalization,
1981–1982

Charlotte Furth

CAMBRIA
PRESS

Amherst, New York

Copyright 2017 Cambria Press

All rights reserved.
Printed in the United States of America

No part of this publication may be reproduced, stored in or introduced into a retrieval system, or transmitted, in any form, or by any means (electronic, mechanical, photocopying, recording, or otherwise), without the prior permission of the publisher.

Photo on front cover is of Weiming Lake
on the campus of Beijing University.

Requests for permission should be directed to
permissions@cambriapress.com, or mailed to:
Cambria Press
100 Corporate Parkway, Suite 128
Amherst, New York 14226, USA

Library of Congress Cataloging-in-Publication Data available.

ISBN 978-1-60497-984-8 (alk. paper)

Table of Contents

List of Figures vii

Preface ix

Chapter 1: Becoming a Historian of China in Cold War America 1

Chapter 2: Arrival— The Friendship Hotel 11

Chapter 3: Fulbrighters Get Oriented 23

Chapter 4: Students and Teachers 35

Chapter 5: Student Stories 47

Chapter 6: American Studies 67

Chapter 7: The Visiting Professor 89

Chapter 8: Spring Fever 103

Chapter 9: Departures 123

Epilogue 131

Acknowledgements ....

Praise for the Book 137

About the Author 141

List of Figures

Figure 1: The author in the People's Republic of China (1982) xii

Figure 2: View from the author's Friendship Hotel apartment (Winter 1981) 20

Figure 3: Inside the author's Friendship Hotel apartment (Winter 1981) 21

Figure 4: Beida Library 33

Figure 5: The "R" Building 34

Figure 6: With students at the Beida Library (Winter 1981) 66

Figure 7: With Monty at the Forbidden City (February 1982) 101

Figure 8: Fan and Bella at Beidaihe beach (June 1982) 120

Figure 9: Official photo of program graduates, Beijing University (June 1982) 121

Figure 10: Photo of the author (2017) 142

Preface

After I finally came back home, I knew right away I wanted to write about that year in China. But in November 1982 it was hard to do. After doctoral research and fifteen years of college teaching as a historian of China, I had finally broken through the "bamboo curtain" imposed by the Cold War. It was exciting to have been among the first Americans to live in the People's Republic after the normalization of relations between our two countries, but my excitement felt suspect to me. All of us, American Fulbright teachers and Chinese students, had spent that year 1981–1982 under political surveillance, and it was clear that private stories could have public repercussions, making self-censorship prudent. Americans were eager for reports from the newly opened mainland, and it was all too easy, even addictive, to relay from the security of the sidelines my year's store of stories: stories of awkward rapprochement that revealed cultural gaps both baffling and comic; some stories of suffering that fed stereotypes of the Maoist Moloch, and others that tempted one to hope for better days to come. Finally, I had my own life to consider—I had said goodbye to husband, daughter, and teaching job, and taken off for a year on my own—a midlife adventure that had to end with the resumption of the intimate rhythms of home. So I settled for showing slides of my travels and relating dinner-party and classroom anecdotes, letting the impulse to more considered reflections slide.

But there was something more in my hesitation. Did I really understand where I had been and what I had seen? For us Americans who had studied China during the decades of the Cold War, the mainland had been a forbidden country, a black box that evoked images of totalitarian horrors or of utopian promise depending on the imagination of the observer. The tiny cadre of American pre-war China specialists had been fractured and scattered by the McCarthyite anti-Communist crusade of the 1950s. From our offshore perches on Taiwan or in Hong Kong, we postwar novices of the 1960s and 1970s had wondered if our fieldwork overseas exposed us to the "real China" or to some colonial outpost. Although many of our studies were supported by the American government's National Defense Education Act, which financed what were called "critical area studies," few of us saw our mission as learning to know the enemy. We had wanted to open up a world, but who knew what we would find?

Coming home at the end of 1982, I knew that in a small way I had been witness to a whole society's hesitant emergence from a traumatic historical transformation. But was this the moment of promise that I wanted it to be? Could I conclude that the revolution with which I had originally sympathized had been worth the terrible sacrifices whose traces I saw all about me? Or, alternatively, could I be confident that we western sojourners were part of a movement of release and innovation sweeping away the bad past? The truth was, I had gone expecting to find answers to these questions, but after over a year living at last among the Chinese I had studied for two decades, I still did not know. Moreover, I had come to realize that the people in Beijing whom I came to know, love, and admire that year did not know either. Some ice was breaking up, but it could easily be only a temporary thaw, while beneath the ice flowed a deep river of history shaping both freeze and thaw according to patterns we were still unable to grasp.

The present is always a fleeting tightrope walk between the unalterable past and the unknown future. My year of opening to China was a time when this perennial instability felt vertiginous to me. As I try to recapture the peculiar novelty of those times it is easier to evoke my impressionable self of 1981 than a discovered world that has the imagined stability of an ethnographic present. I can recover its presence—access it now as new—largely because in the intervening years it has been as if I had forgotten most of it. But it was not Proustian memory tricks that led me back so much as the letters I wrote home to my husband, unfiltered field notes of the puzzles, excitements, and frustrations that consumed me day by day. Today's readers, however, will bring the filters of their own historical memories to a narrative that may seem to evoke an almost-vanished world.

Figure 1. The author in the People's Republic of China (1982).

Opening to China

Chapter 1

Becoming a Historian of China in Cold War America

The path that led me to China began in 1957, when the Russians launched their famous Sputnik space capsule and heated up US–Soviet Cold War competition. When I arrived at Stanford in 1959 to begin doctoral work in history, I learned that the US government, through the National Defense Education Act, was offering fellowships to students willing to explore "critical area studies." Asia, Africa, and Latin America (as well as the Soviet Union) were to be targets of scholarship aimed at expanding America's global reach. I jumped at the chance to switch from French history to the history of China.

What motivated me? The more conservative of the congressmen who dangled this big pot of money in front of young scholars probably thought they were buying experts so that Americans could expand global influence and know our enemies. But I was drawn to the idea that a world-historical civilization had been basically invisible in my education. For an American to study France was to tend a garden; to study China was to explore a wilderness. The context of the Cold War added contemporary relevance, for American ignorance was reinforced by our refusal to grant diplomatic recognition to the People's Republic of China (PRC). With diplomacy, cultural exchange, commerce, and journalism cut off after the establishment of the PRC in 1950, what could we really know about the new society the Communists were building? I remember being particularly struck by the news stories that were flooding the American press about China's Great Leap Forward (1958–1960). Among accounts of massive construction projects carried out using manual labor one photograph struck me particularly: an aerial view of hundreds of Chinese carrying buckets of earth on shoulder poles, excavating by hand the reservoir that would bring water to the city of Beijing. Its caption read, "A Nation of Blue Ants." I felt that something was deeply wrong with that picture. The liberal internationalist in me wanted to expose it, but this would require another sort of digging.

So for those of us who entered the expanding field of Chinese studies in the late 1950s and 1960s, Mao's revolution hulked over the landscape from the start. It had already left scars on our immediate predecessors, the small cadre of diplomats, journalists, and scholars who had advised our military in the China theater of World War II. Many had admired the Communist anti-Japanese resistance and had reported frankly on Nationalist failures. For this they were vilified by Senator Joseph McCarthy and the notorious House Un-American Activities Committee in the early 1950s. In a national atmosphere of anti-Communist hysteria, the experts who knew China best were deemed responsible for "the loss of China." Careers were ruined, some people left the country, and the field's major professional organization, the Association for Asian Studies (AAS), nervously retreated from political controversy. But as the United States slid into full engagement in the Vietnam War after 1965, the policy vacuum among China experts was filled by a new cohort of angry dissenters, opponents of a conflict that seemed eerily to recapitulate the earlier civil war on the Chinese mainland and that was fueling a youth rebellion in both politics and culture at home. Politics revived within the AAS in the form of heated debates among the board of directors and on panels at the association's annual meetings. A splinter group of activists formed the Committee of Concerned Asian Scholars (CCAS) and published an anti-imperialist journal opposing the war and calling for normalization of diplomatic relations; in addition, this group was highly sympathetic to Maoist revolutionary policies.

Though most of us, myself included, lacked the Marxist edge of this radical vanguard, in the 1960s we found it easy to think of the Maoist revolution favorably. First of all, there was the simple fact that, in an age of decolonization and national liberations worldwide, it was the Communist revolution that in 1949 had established China as independent, sovereign, and ideologically modern. In Europe, where Communist parties remained legitimate, Stalinism had discredited the Soviet Union as a model, and some erstwhile Soviet sympathizers looked to China for alternatives. The Maoist regime was there to stay, and the historian's question was to understand how this had happened.

I followed the mainstream of pioneer American researchers in the agenda set by Harvard's senior expert, John Fairbank, to investigate "China's response to the West" in the nineteenth and early twentieth centuries. We scholars debated: was the seeming inertia and stagnation of the late Qing empire due to Western imperialism, embodied in treaty ports authorized by gunboat diplomacy, or did its roots lie in a crippling cultural conservatism? In either case, it was a narrative of Chinese failure. As we investigated internal reform movements that faltered over and over again, we paid sympathetic attention to the 1919 "May Fourth" anti-imperialist and cultural reform movement where a splinter group of radicals had founded the Chinese Communist Party. As mid-century peasant uprisings, warlord conflicts, and Japanese invasion created internal division and chaos, the decision many Chinese had made to throw in their lot with Mao's peasant revolution seemed reasonable. The victory of the People's Liberation Army ended what the Chinese today still call "the century of humiliation."

With this as its foundation, the picture of Mao's China I sketched for my American students was of a new beginning, in which many utopian projects of modernity were given another chance. The mass campaigns of the 1950s aimed to destroy "feudal" class hierarchy, redistribute land to the peasants, emancipate women, improve public health, build schools to promote mass literacy, and spread the benefits of science and technology throughout society. Those who pointed out the coercive methods and human costs of these campaigns could be identified with the defeated rump Republic of China on Taiwan, an American protectorate that itself was a military dictatorship during those years. In a time of hope, I aligned those critics with the reflexive anti-Communism of America during the Cold War. Whatever doubts were planted by stories of the revolution's victims, I continued to wish the Chinese people and their new government well.

And China *was* different. While the "area studies" project in Soviet affairs withered, we new China hands saw that revolutionary China, with its mobilized peasantry and pride in national liberation, was no Soviet satellite. This became even clearer as the Chinese split with their Soviet allies in the late 1950s and dedicated themselves to Mao's independent path. I and others teaching about modern Chinese history explained how the "century of humiliation," including the Sino–Japanese War, had ensured Communist victory. But as one mass campaign succeeded another—for agricultural collectivization and a "great leap" in economic development; for "thought reform" and "socialist education" targeting educated elites—things became a little puzzling. Using official reports of these movements, we tried to understand the reasoning behind them. Chinese claims for egalitarian goals and material progress seemed impressive. Then after the late 1950s, when the Chinese Communist Party openly split between the "red" Maoists and more moderate "experts" or "revisionists," things became more puzzling. In 1966, the split deepened into a chasm. The Maoists called for "Cultural Revolution" and student Red Guards were soon carrying on tumultuous mass campaigns against "the four olds"—old ideas, old culture, old customs, old habits—which soon split their ranks and society at large into furiously contentious factions.

Still, for us western observers, the Cultural Revolution as an embodiment of China's difference took place in the context of the global ferment of the 1960s. Student-led movements rocked Europe in 1968—extending to street actions, strikes, and even assassinations. In the United States, protests against the Vietnam War culminated in a bitter primary battle for the Democratic nomination for president. In Chicago, where the nominating convention was being held, there were riots in the street; and the assassinations of Martin Luther King and Robert Kennedy that same year deepened the sense of national crisis.

Were China's Red Guard student campaigns against the Party leadership similar protests—signs of populist revolt against state authority? Did the movement within the Communist Party pitting "reds" against "experts" expose the way that intellectual and academic authority everywhere generates its own forms of privilege and social inequality? Hadn't our own elites led us into the Vietnam quagmire? To my students these issues were clearly relevant to the cultural and political crises that were engulfing the United States during the antiwar movement. From Andy Warhol's iconic color portrait of the Chairman, to the "Little Red Book" of Mao quotations that Black Panthers carried around the streets of Oakland, Mao's China symbolized something aspirational for many. Revolutionary utopianism was enhanced when it was embodied in a still-hidden Orient of Western imagination.

When the possibility of normalization finally developed in 1972, its architects, Nixon and Kissinger, were thinking strategically: how to triangulate the Sino–Soviet rivalry and ease the US withdrawal from Vietnam? But we Asia scholars thrilled at the chance to penetrate the mystery and possibly answer two decades' worth of accumulated questions about the New China. We were not the only ones with positive hopes. Washington policymakers were elated by their diplomatic coup, businessmen dusted off long-shelved plans for a market, and the public went through one of its periodic spurts of Orientalist fascination with all things Chinese. Then, as progress towards the restoration of full diplomatic relations stalled in the mid-1970s, people competed for the limited access made possible by the Chinese government's policy of controlled visits by official delegations and Soviet-style "socialist tourism." Groups of twenty to forty carefully selected individuals were shepherded through two-to-three-week group tours according to a fixed itinerary that featured model institutions of the New China, political briefings, and a smattering of famous monuments. I was not well-known enough to be included on one of the tours arranged for senior historians of China, but I did wangle a place on a two-week tour organized by the Southern California chapter of the US–China Peoples' Friendship Association, a long-standing group of American Communists who had broken with the Soviet Union about fifteen years earlier.

It was spring 1976, early May to be exact. We tourists had all been selected as Americans friendly to China, and the group included assorted commune dwellers, environmentalists from the Pacific Northwest, anti-Vietnam War activists, and a couple of old socialists who had actually once visited the USSR. But most of us were younger and middle-class—these tours were not cheap—and the fact that I was the lone China specialist didn't matter much. Early on in Beijing, an inept young man named Sam, whom someone had designated as leader, called us together as a group, with the aim of ensuring that we presented a united front to our hosts. The group quickly divided between a few radicals who wanted us to defer to the Chinese in all matters—and the rest of us.

Our internal divisions were unimportant in the end. The group was constrained by the tight schedule, by the determination of our guides and local hosts to keep to an assigned script, and also by our own ignorance and occasional stupefaction. Based on reports from earlier visitors I knew to expect a menu of model institutions—agricultural communes, industrial workplaces, schools, neighborhood associations, and hospitals. We would be taken by bus from our hotel to a selected location and turned over to the foreign affairs cadre of the unit, who would march us through the site, ending in a conference room with antimacassars on the chairs and cups of tea at each place setting. At this point the cadre would speak, sometimes at length, about the proletarian virtues of his organization. Questions were then solicited, but those that challenged the wisdom presented quickly came to seem worse than rude—I felt they were actively unkind. Our hosts were performing for themselves as well as for us. It was as if their hypersensitivity itself was evidence of how badly they needed our approval.

Little things attracted my notice. The model commune near Beijing was even poorer than I had expected. When I paused in the main courtyard, attracted by a frog in the catch basin of an outdoor faucet, an old woman came up and proudly turned it on. It took me some minutes to realize she was showing off their new running water. At the newly opened Shengli oil field in central Shandong, we were introduced to an all-female team of well diggers. They were complying with a directive to open complex industrial jobs to women, but they were clearly terrified at their dangerous assignment. Surgery with acupuncture anesthesia was certainly remarkable, even as I could not help noticing the exposed cables snaking across the floor, bringing electrical power to the operating theater. Most surreal was to listen to kindergarten children chanting a ditty against the "counter-revolutionary revisionist Deng Xiaoping" when Deng had been officially restored to the ruling Politburo by party leaders only a few months before.

I saw pretty quickly that our guides were nervous. In spite of the uniform dress, there were clear class and cultural differences between the articulate female guides and hostesses, most young and speaking good English, and the weathered and taciturn older males who were introduced everywhere as peasant activists. These men said as little as possible and avoided eye contact. In fact, events soon revealed that my tour had coincided with a moment of national crisis. Zhou Enlai had died in January 1976, and a huge demonstration commemorating him—a protest disguised as a ceremony of mourning—had taken place in Tiananmen Square in April. In May, we tourists arrived in the midst of a last campaign of the Cultural Revolution, as "reds" struggled to oust Zhou's ally, the "revisionist" Deng Xiaoping, and position themselves to secure power when the Chairman eventually died. Mao Zedong would die in October of that same year. A month later his wife Jiang Qing and her associated Cultural Revolution radicals would be arrested, and in 1977 they would be put on trial as the "Gang of Four." No wonder our hosts were on edge.

I went home glad I had finally seen a little of the landscape—the sights, smells, and sounds of the mainland, plus a few historic monuments like the Forbidden City and the Great Wall—but most impressed with the power of a propaganda system to enforce uniformity among all who dealt with foreign guests. "Socialist tourism" made spontaneous interactions almost impossible. In the next several years revelations of the horrors of the Cultural Revolution accumulated, and it became clearer that we visitors had floated as if in a glass balloon over a devastated landscape. Everyone was being forced to rethink the revolution's history, Mao's place as its presiding deity, and the path forward.

Full normalization of diplomatic relations in 1979 was part of this process. It had been authorized by Deng Xiaoping, Mao's successor as de facto Communist Party chief, who called for openness to the outside world, for economic and cultural exchange, and for a spirit of pragmatism in economic development policies. Revival of the American government's Fulbright program, which had been sending scholars and teachers abroad all over the world since the 1950s, was one of many academic exchanges now extended to the PRC. We scholars would at last be able to sojourn in China for months or even years; archives would be open to us, and we might be part of a new era of cooperation between our peoples.

CHAPTER 2

ARRIVAL—
THE FRIENDSHIP HOTEL

First, out of the window of the airplane from Tokyo, I saw a brown landscape of patchwork fields evocative of China's legendary "yellow earth." Then darkness fell, the plane landed on an otherwise empty runway, and we passengers walked across a tarmac to Beijing's new international airport terminal, now boasting baggage carousels far too capacious for the luggage off our lone jetliner. I looked for the new mural I had been told about that depicted chastely nude minority beauties bathing in a spring stream. It had caused a sensation when unveiled on the occasion of the opening of the airport in 1979. But I was too late. It had been screened over by officials regretting the boldness of having commissioned such a work.

In China as elsewhere, the first local encounter of a visitor crossing an international border is likely to be with a customs official. I had brought in a number of gifts that Chinese friends and acquaintances living in Los Angeles, not trusting the mails, wanted delivered to their relatives in Beijing. An electric shaver, a pocket calculator, a tape recorder, and two wristwatches, still in their store packaging, revealed themselves in my luggage. And, I learned quickly from the customs inspector, these foreign-made consumer goods were subject to import restrictions. The designated recipients could come to the airport and collect them after paying a tax. No, I could not pay the tax on their behalf. And so my presents disappeared and I got my first lesson in smuggling.

Otherwise my heavy load of baggage, typewriter, portable radio, and books was unexceptionable. A taciturn chauffeur identified himself and loaded me into a nondescript black car for the twenty-mile drive into the city. Once we had left the airport, the driver simply turned off his headlights, which unnerved me, but of course there were hardly any oncoming cars on the road. In the dark the moonlit shadows of spindly rows of newly planted trees bordered invisible agricultural fields, and if there were peasant houses nearby, no lights revealed their presence.

The transition from rural to urban space was a sudden one, marked by additional lanes flanking multistory structures in cinderblock modern style, and widely spaced streetlights forming pools of dim illumination. Two or three men squatted around each lamp, using the light to play cards or just to smoke and chat. But beyond these few islands of human activity all was darkness and silence. Where were the people? Then suddenly we pulled through the gates of a huge walled compound and onto the grounds of the Friendship Hotel, the huge complex designed in the 1950s to house foreigners employed by Chinese state agencies. The Soviet experts who had originally filled it were long gone, but Americans were now joining the assortment of itinerant cosmopolitans who continued to serve as official "foreign experts" for the government. It was to be my home for the next year.

Arrival—The Friendship Hotel

By light of day the following morning, the Friendship Hotel revealed itself as far more than a "hotel"—it was a compound of a dozen or more large buildings on an enclosed campus a half mile square. I found myself in a fourth floor walkup apartment in one of the many residential blocks that dominated the landscape. The main room accommodated a desk, table, bookcase, three easy chairs, and a big wardrobe, while a tiny bedroom with two twin beds adjoined. I knew enough to realize that though a kitchenette consisting of a two-burner hotplate, a tiny sink, and a wooden drain board was too rudimentary for an American to find attractive, a full bath—even with cracked and stained porcelain on both tub and flush toilet—was a luxury few in China enjoyed. (A sign said that hot water was available mornings and evenings.)

And it turned out I had housekeeping service! Early the next morning a middle-aged man appeared with a thermos of boiled hot water for drinking and tea. Old Sun was talkative, and I could even understand most of his Chinese. Leaning on his broom, he chatted away about how wonderful my digs were: everything had been painted (beige), and there was even wallpaper (blue and white flowers)! When I ungraciously mentioned that I had seen a couple of cockroaches in the kitchenette, he was not offended. "It can't be helped," he announced cheerfully. "They come in through the drainage pipes and walls. The Russians brought them." He implied that you had to admire cockroaches for being indestructible, but for another leftover from the Russians, he had a solution. For a small sum he could supply electrical connectors for the Soviet-style plug outlets—a nice little sideline business.

Sun made me feel like an army officer enjoying the services of an orderly. I wondered idly whether he was a People's Liberation Army veteran. It would be a secure job for a reliable countryman, who could be counted on to provide good service and also act as eyes and ears reporting on untoward behavior on the part of foreign guests. But as far as I could tell his contribution to my life at the Friendship Hotel turned out to be entirely benign.

Outside my window lay a courtyard, made dusty by the bare ground but supplied with trees and shrubs. In the early morning martial reveille music blared out from the public loudspeakers of nearby apartment blocks, and during the daytime traffic noise from the boulevard beyond the walls could be heard. But in the evening the courtyard filled with the voices of Hotel resident children playing in the twilight, while the traffic dwindled to no more than the *clop clop* of an occasional horse cart. Cement walks led to the public buildings for Hotel residents. These included an auditorium/movie theater, a beauty salon, a laundry and small "notions" shop, even an Olympic-sized outdoor swimming pool, though hardly anyone seemed to use it. Above all, we were supplied with a grand dining room, well staffed in the style of a big old fashioned hotel, which served delicious meals three times a day. I wasn't going to have to cope with my hot plates at all.

The dining room was where residents of the Friendship Hotel mingled, and where the character of the establishment gradually became clear. Ours was for residents who spoke English and other European languages; at set hours the buffet menus offered Chinese–Mediterranean fusion cuisine that I came to enjoy, once I adjusted to the fact that I would never be served cheese, salads, or sandwiches. (We were told that the head chef had formerly served the Cuban embassy.) Diners clumped by language, with English predominating, but French, German, and Eastern European tongues could also be heard. Somewhere at the other end of the campus, ten minutes away and beyond the perimeter of our daily rounds, there was a separate

Arrival—The Friendship Hotel

compound just for Japanese residents, and beyond them a terra incognita where visiting foreign scientists gathered.

All of us, it seemed, were "foreign experts," classified as employees of the Chinese government engaged in officially approved tasks of technical assistance and foreign cultural exchange. Officials referred to us all as "friends of China." In my wing of the establishment, most worked to produce the western-language versions of the PRC's official publications, while some served as language teachers in local colleges. The Korean War had driven most western experts away from China by the mid-1950s, and after the collapse of the Sino–Soviet alliance the Russians also departed. But an assortment of European international leftists and unemployed brain workers continued to come and go through the decade of the Cultural Revolution and after. Most intriguing were the old socialists who had thrown in their lot with the PRC in the early days of Communist rule, who had been celebrity "friends of China" until the Cultural Revolution had toppled them, along with the orthodox Leninism that they had espoused. Permanent residents of the PRC, a few had returned to their apartments in the Friendship Hotel after being officially rehabilitated. But they rarely came to the dining room, and they were not talking about their lives.

For me, being housed in the Friendship Hotel soon revealed itself as fun. American scholars and researchers were a novelty in Beijing in 1981, but normalization was cracking open the door. The Hotel was mandated as an alternative to having the new trickle of visitors try to find housing on their own in the city or be hosted by universities unsure of their roles in post-Mao China. In addition to us four Fulbright teachers, several other "China hand" researchers and professors had found ways to secure "foreign expert" assignments; a few graduate students housed at local universities found ways to be invited to dinner on a regular basis, and Fred Wakeman, an eminent China historian from Berkeley, was in residence as chair of a new official Committee on Scholarly Communication with the People's Republic of China. At times the gossipy dinner table resembled an informal Berkeley faculty club.

At other times I was reminded that Sino-foreign contact zones extended far beyond westerners. Japanese, invisible on a daily basis, showed up for occasional Hotel-sponsored outings by bus to nearby tourist destinations. The Hotel had an outdoor roof garden and bar which was still open in the mild early September evenings. At night, drinking beer, we found Africans. At this point the informal segregation of the Friendship Hotel assumed an eerie aspect, given that we saw no Africans in our dining hall or other public spaces. In late September a European woman acquaintance told me that these folks gave great Saturday night parties, and invited me along. It was in a distant compound that felt like a village within a village, and the party went on all night with disco music and dancing. The residents—from places like Tanzania, Zambia, and the Sudan—were all on Chinese government stipends. Most were students of technology and engineering and had signed on to programs that committed them to up to five years of training. The puritanism, discipline, and intellectual snobbery of the Chinese elite were clearly driving them nuts—and the few Chinese girls who joined this party were engaged in risky behavior. Because many of the men, who greatly outnumbered the women, were eagerly looking for girlfriends, I didn't go back.

The staff treated foreign experts like privileged visitors. They arranged bus tours to local historical sites—the Great Wall, the Western Hills, the Qing imperial tombs, and beyond. They offered tickets to the visiting western classical music concerts and art exhibits that were beginning to be booked in the capital, and to an array of

Arrival—The Friendship Hotel

Chinese entertainments revived as the Cultural Revolution's ban on "feudal and bourgeois" art began to ease. There was opera, ballet, circus acts, and the standard variety shows that featured accordion-stomping folk dances and robust baritones singing arias left over from the Soviet era. Residents could take *taiji* classes, learn calligraphy, and go to Chinese movies in the compound auditorium every Friday night. We were even supplied with earphones and halting simultaneous translations in several languages. There were weeks when the choice of entertainments was overwhelming. Did I want to go to an Egyptian dance concert? Visit the medieval Liao-dynasty tombs? How about a public lecture from a visiting European scholar on the famous Buddhist cave temples at Dunhuang?

But the comfort zone of the Friendship Hotel ensured that the life of a "friend of China" would be a segregated one. The entry gates were guarded by PLA soldiers in uniform who checked the identity of every Chinese visitor, which assured that visitors would be few. Throughout the Mao era, similar socialist "gated communities" had provided high officials security and luxuries hidden from the eyes of ordinary citizens. Similarly the Chinese audience members at the foreign-oriented cultural events at my disposal had gotten tickets though some unadvertised patronage process parallel to the one that served me. This system that concealed privilege and protected power holders clashed with my American hopes for open communication and a chance to know the Chinese on an informal basis.

To step outside the Friendship Hotel was to enter a vast cityscape of grey, blue, and brown, and to join the stream of buses and bicycles moving like a school of fish in a sea of traffic, all keeping the same measured pace. Along White Stone Bridge Boulevard between Purple Bamboo Park to the south and Beijing University about three miles to the north, the divided highway was lined with other compounds, each one like the Friendship Hotel a separate socialist "unit" (*danwei*) of residence and employment, providing total communities for citizens. In a city dominated by such *danwei*, there was no room for private apartment buildings. Beyond an open-air market across the street where one could buy a few seasonal fruits and vegetables and get shoes and bicycles repaired, there were few visible private shops, restaurants, or places of entertainment. The big state-department stores downtown would sell a foreigner a ready-made khaki or navy blue jacket, but we needed bicycles—scarce, expensive, and available only after many trips and long lines at the downtown Friendship Store, which dealt exclusively in foreign exchange currency. This currency—yuan available only in exchange for dollars—gave foreigners privileged access to scarce consumer goods, though from the crowds of customers thronging the aisles it was clear some Chinese were able to game the system.

On our Chinese-made "flying pigeon" bikes (one speed), we quickly learned to swim in Chinese traffic, partially camouflaged by our blue or khaki jackets, though our shoes as much as our faces were a giveaway. Bicyclists, each in an independent bubble of space, sped up or slowed down in response to the mass pressure of other riders. Buses and trucks complicated our stately progress through the roundabout street crossings between the hotel and the university campus, as they crosscut other traffic with impunity. Motor vehicles may have been few by California standards, but they gave no quarter, honking as we bicycle riders swerved fore and aft to escape and still reach our destinations in one piece. We also had to watch for dust motes in the eyes or an occasional patch of donkey shit. Amazingly, all this gradually came to seem normal.

On the streets we were part of a Beijing that was collective without contact. In this sober cityscape the range of colors was muted and the

Arrival—The Friendship Hotel

range of emotions tended toward neutral. Taciturn workaday crowds pushed and shoved to board the rackety buses where seats were always full; passengers carefully avoided eye contact while their bodies were pressed against one another. There were no advertisements, neon signs, storefront displays, or billboards beyond a few giant Maoist propaganda posters already beginning to look a little derelict. Most temples were closed. Parks and monuments had visitors, but except for the city zoo (a rare treat!) they were decorous places—OK for morning *taiji* and Sunday family strolls, but where nobody walked a dog, picnicked, or trod on the grass. Were the young couples sitting awkwardly on a park bench courting? How could you tell? After hyperstimulated California, I found the absence of commercialism refreshing. To many returning Chinese like my Fulbright colleague Phebe Chao, who remembered her Shanghai childhood in the 1950s, the drabness represented a criminal leveling of society. And I did have to wonder how citizens of the PRC raised in such a stripped-down environment saw the world. Had social and aesthetic possibilities simply been erased, or was there a richer, perhaps more familiar, private life going on behind the scenes? These were questions I hoped my students would help me answer.

Figure 2. View from the author's Friendship Hotel apartment (Winter 1981).

Figure 3. Inside the author's Friendship Hotel apartment (Winter 1981).

Chapter 3

Fulbrighters Get Oriented

Now we Americans were back. Jimmy Carter's official normalization of relations in January 1979 had brought with it a new fully staffed Beijing embassy and a tiny group of American reporters housed in a downtown hotel. President Carter's Committee on Scholarly Communication with the People's Republic would facilitate exchanges, among them the Fulbright program that had been suspended in 1949 and shut down when the outbreak of the Korean War led to a blizzard of accusations that the remaining scholars were CIA spies. I was a teaching Fulbright scholar, one of four in the third year of the revived program. The other three were all specialists in American literature: Phebe Chao from Bennington, Michael Yetman from Purdue, and Priscilla Oaks from California State University at Fullerton. Whereas the pioneer Fulbright professors of late 1979 and 1980 had been English-as-a-Second Language specialists, we were assigned a more ambitious agenda of introducing "American Studies" to young Chinese academics destined to be professors of English.

At a reception at the American embassy a couple of nights after our arrival, we got an introduction to officials from the Ministry of Education, still uneasy about the new turn in foreign relations. About a half-dozen officials appeared, smiled a lot, and departed promptly after one hour. I could not tell whether they actually drank the warm gin and tonics being served. It was clear that the standard pattern of senior Fulbright scholars elsewhere in the world—a teaching scholar is hosted by an academic department at a university—was "inconvenient." We would teach young scholars brought to Beida from around the country in a special program designed to operate outside the regular university structure. But no one was explicit about the basic work load required of us, or the content of our classroom offerings, and here the advice offered by our American embassy hosts was also vague. "The Chinese prefer ambiguity," John Thomson, the Press and Cultural Affairs officer who had set up the Fulbright exchange, told me, but also "don't be afraid to be firm in negotiation."

The designation of the Fulbright scholars as "foreign expert" teachers clearly solved one class of problem; it established us as official "friends of China" and placed us in the segregated establishment designed for such persons. It also made us employees of the Chinese government. To drive home the point, the authorities supplemented our American-paid Fulbright stipends with the Chinese foreign experts' salary appropriate to our ranks, delivered to us every month in bills in a plain envelope. My Chinese monthly pay, 750 yuan, was almost three times that of a Chinese college professor.

I never found out who conducted the final negotiations about our work loads and schedules. Somehow Phebe Chao was delegated to explain to the rest of us that we each would have six hours of classroom teaching per week, divided between one large two-hour lecture and two smaller two-hour seminars with fifteen students each. The program would also accommodate six Beida postgraduate students, who would attend our classes and seminars as auditors. We faculty were to volunteer office hours as an add-on. The embassy staff assured us that we would have total control of course content at all times and would order the books we desired through diplomatic post. Finally, the Chinese authorities insisted that audiovisual materials be scheduled outside of regular classroom hours. There was to be no shortchanging of student–faculty contact time by showing movies.

For us Fulbright teachers, the sanctioned contact zone was the Beijing University classroom. I was excited to arrive at the campus of this university which had been a famous catalyst for modern innovation and reform for almost a century. The site fascinated me with its traces of a layered history. From the eighteenth century all that remained of a famous high official's palace and gardens was Weiming Lake, encircled by a wooded path overlooking a small island inhabited only by birds and ducks. When the nearby Yuanmingyuan—the old imperial summer palace—had been looted and burned by British troops in 1860, the official's estate too was swept away. The only modern tribute to this lost grandeur—the concrete lakeside pagoda built in 1924 and camouflaging a water tower—could still inspire a ghostly enchantment in those who on misty days followed its reflections in the water. Then there was the quaint neo-traditional architecture favored by the Presbyterian founders of the original campus, the elite private Yenching University—stout concrete buildings topped with green glazed tile roofs with curved eaves and decorative wooden supporting struts. At the southwest end of the campus an enclave of two-story single-family faculty houses built in the early twentieth century was half-hidden by large trees and unkempt shrubbery—left over from landscaping originally designed to make Anglo-American missionary teachers and their families feel at home.

With the Communist takeover in 1950, the modern Beijing University moved from downtown to this imperial/colonial retreat, with a resulting decline in architectural interest. Soviet-style utilitarianism triumphed in a central quadrangle dominated by a multistory midcentury modern central library building, in front of which stood a giant statue of Mao Zedong, flanked by ginkgo trees. In September 1981, people were anxious to erase the visible scars of the Cultural Revolution, which they blamed for dilapidated conditions on campus. Renovations were underway everywhere, as workers clambered over bamboo scaffolding to effect changes that seemed to me barely even cosmetic. What I liked best, and what made me tolerant of the underlying shabbiness, was the casual, ramshackle natural beauty of a campus that was actually spacious, a rare phenomenon in Beijing. The ginkgo trees flanking Mao's statue were just beginning to show their autumn gold; there was an old apple orchard near my office building, and in many places the grass—which no one had thought to mow or trim—hummed with insects: grasshoppers, crickets, praying mantises. Pockmarks from the armed battles of the Cultural Revolution may have still defaced student dorms, but in the sunlight of Indian summer, nature turned neglect into rustic charm.

Two Beida officials were in charge of providing us with what we needed to function. They would supervise our work, take care of our problems, and be responsible to the university vice president and the Ministry of Education beyond. Ma Shiyi was a short, compactly built man in his late forties. His lips curved naturally upwards, suggesting a face smiling in repose, and he complemented this with real smiles and a genial air of welcome, as though he knew we all shared common goals and that all would go well with the program. Before 1949, as a young man from Shandong, Ma had studied at a Jesuit academy not because his family was Christian, but because they thought it offered the best education. However, he rejected an offer to study at a Christian seminary in Germany and had thrown in his lot with the Chinese revolution at home. Ma's deputy, Guan Yushan, a generation older and far more fluent in English, beamed at us with scarcely repressed glee as he let us know that he had worked with the Americans before 1949. He had been a basketball coach back when the Beida campus was a missionary college run by American Presbyterians, and during World War II he had been attached to General Stilwell's office. During the 1950s, the two men had cemented their friendship as they were both assigned to Beida's sports research and teaching program, which was managed in collaboration with Tsinghua, the premier technical university next door. Now they had offices in the Beida central library, where Guan was in charge of the tiny English language reading room that had just been supplied with books by the Americans, and that was open for use a ridiculously small numbers of hours each week. It seemed both had had difficulties during the Cultural Revolution but had recently been promoted to be part of a new administration dedicated to restoring academic programs. Whereas Guan recalled the earlier era of Sino-American cooperation before 1949, Ma seemed a party loyalist reassuring us that the socialist revolution was back on track. Their assistant, Zhou, was a glum young man who claimed to be on the English faculty at Beida, which seemed surprising given that he was an indifferent student. But he had survived the Cultural Revolution, which suggested other talents—perhaps a powerful patron or an ability to keep his head down.

These were the Chinese officials who had picked the four of us out of the larger pool of American scholars who had applied to the Fulbright office in Washington, DC. What had made them choose us, I wondered, and why had my fellow Fulbright teachers applied to come? What we Americans were looking for did not seem too difficult to guess. Tall, lanky, with thick blond hair, Michael Yetman was passionate about Hawthorne, Melville, and Whitman, and he had uprooted his Midwestern wife and three children for a China adventure that might recapture some of the excitement of the 1960s and reenergize him as a creative writer. Priscilla Oaks was another refugee from the 1960s; she was an unmarried, outspoken feminist who had escaped the routines of mass higher education at California State University Fullerton to come to China the previous year to teach English language in a technical college in Shanghai. Clearly, she did not want to go home.

As for Phebe Chao, her Rubenesque figure, great mane of flowing black hair, and round, penetrating black eyes did not fit Chinese feminine stereotypes. But in fact she was the granddaughter of a pioneer Chinese woman doctor trained in Wisconsin in the early twentieth century. Phebe herself had been born in China and had lived in Shanghai until the age of twelve, when the revolution drove her family abroad. I had to find out about this background on my own because Phebe did not tell her colleagues much about herself. For companionship she had a partner, a mild bear-like man named Roger Sorkin who said he was a musician. No one asked whether they were married. But Phebe was a native speaker of Chinese, and she had clear claims to a more intimate relationship with our hosts and with the realities of the Chinese revolution than any of the rest of us.

What was I doing in this group? My job was to introduce American history and sociology. In my letter of application I had concocted a speciously plausible narrative about my experience teaching Chinese history to Americans as preparation for presenting American history to Chinese. But in fact I had never taken a college-level American history class, and my high school education in the American South of the 1950s was hardly foundation for anything useful in the 1980s. Having been selected, I was gambling that I could wing it, supplied with some textbooks and a hastily assembled syllabus I could read as I went along. (A dozen years of heavy undergraduate teaching at California State University Long Beach prepared one to improvise like this.) I did not confess the extent of my ignorance to Mr. Ma, but when I asked why they had selected me, he said simply, "you have some knowledge of China." Later I learned they had been turned down by a "real" American historian before they looked to me.

So there we were, four unlikely colleagues, none from highly elite American institutions. Our agendas differed widely, but it did seem that our Chinese supervisors valued some prior exposure to China and Chinese people over other criteria for the assignment at hand. Later that year, some embassy gossip suggested another concern. Diane Johnston, who had succeeded John Thomson as supervisor of the Fulbright program, revealed that Mr. Ma had been criticized for being too easygoing with the previous year's group of Fulbright professors. Some said he had been too quick to indulge their thirst for touristic outings in chauffeur-driven state cars. But I learned more indirectly that in addition two male professors had caused a scandal by having affairs with Chinese women, and one had even flown home with his inamorata, leaving his wife and children behind in Beijing for the authorities to deal with as best they could. Possibly someone decided that this time it was safer to go with female professors.

Offices and classrooms for the Fulbright group were housed in a grimly functional cement block structure formerly dedicated to Russian language studies and still known as the "R" building. The classrooms, with their high ceilings, unwashed casement windows and cement walls and floors, made it feel a little like teaching at the bottom of a well. The few ancient steam radiators mounted around the walls suggested that the volume of enclosed air would never be warmed enough to let us shed our outdoor clothing in winter.

Beyond this building and the library where Ma and Guan had their offices, the rest of the campus, faculty and students, were so many blank walls to me. There were no maps or guides to the grounds. Buildings were marked by numbers only, and office doors were not only normally shut, but bore no names of their occupants. I never saw a class schedule, for our group or any other department at the university. If you belonged there, you figured out what was going on. Others did not need to know.

The following is an early example of my figuring out what one needs to know. At the embassy reception I had been briefly introduced to Beida historian Qi Wenying, a professor specializing in colonial America, who could serve to connect me to the university's history program. She was visibly disappointed at my poor spoken Chinese but invited me to her class. It might be good language practice for me, I agreed. I went to the class at the appointed time. No one was there. A student saw me and told me that the class had been changed to Saturday afternoon, and suggested I try the History Department office. "It's in the second courtyard." I went. One unmarked door along the corridor was ajar, and an old man inside was busily writing. As I was hesitating about whether to disturb him, a woman came along the corridor. I told her I was looking for Professor Qi's office. "Can't you reach her at home? "she said. I said I didn't have an address. She went into the open office and asked the old man for me. It turned out he was the staff assistant for the department and after some suspicious looks, he said he would take a note from me to Qi at her home in the faculty housing quarter. But it was now noon and past time for lunch and a rest. Would I come back with my note at two o'clock? Wandering around campus to kill time, I soon met a student of mine, and when I explained my predicament, she said "I will find Professor Qi and deliver your note." It would be easy, she said. "This afternoon is political study, and everyone will be on campus." I wrote and gave her the note; the next day she reported back that she had been unable to find Qi, and so she had taken the note back to the history office, where she had also learned that the time change for Qi's class was for one week only. (As for Professor Qi, after one or two tries I gave up auditing her lectures, but she did invite me to her home for Thanksgiving dinner, a Beida novelty. (In a tiny living room and kitchen crammed with about twenty people, we all rolled *jiaozi* dumplings. There was no turkey.)

In fact one key to figuring out what is going on, I gradually realized, is to understand that in fact all students in each department follow a common curriculum, and that all classes start at 8:30 a.m., break at noon for two and a half hours, and resume from 2:30 p.m. to 5:00 p.m. Early on I tried going back to my office at 12:45, but the door was locked shut. Even if I got in, no student would show up until 2:30 at least. So lunch hour was proving a problem. So was lunch. When we asked, "where do we eat lunch on campus?" Mr. Ma looked worried. The senior cadres' dining room, where Ma and Guan ate, was obviously out of the question. He said he didn't know about the Beida teachers' dining hall. As for the students, there was a foreign students' dining room but the food there was indifferent, he said, and the Chinese students' dining hall had the worst food of all. We eventually were assigned a niche in a low-ranking faculty/staff cafeteria where, using coupons supplied by Ma, we could get a subsidized steam-tray buffet. My impulse to protest this system of privilege faded after one meal at the student dining hall, where the meat disappeared onto the plates of the first hundred students in line, leaving most with a bowl of coarse grey-pink rice topped with pork gristle and cabbage. It took about five minutes to wolf down this fare, and conversation was impossible.

It gradually became clear that this fixed hierarchy of rank and quality of rations placed our Fulbright students at the bottom, along with ordinary undergraduates. No wonder that in my morning lecture class students started to get restless as the hour passed 11:30. They also bunked in the grim Beida undergraduate dormitories, four-story cinderblock warrens divided into rooms each housing four persons in double-decker bunks with washrooms and toilets down the hall. For showers they were expected to go to one of the nearby public bathhouses. I never visited any of them in these living quarters, but some of my students described them to me with grim irony, laughing at my dismay. Where the Friendship Hotel provided us teachers with accommodations that amounted to real luxury in the China of 1981, the students—most of them still young but no longer adolescents—were accepting what Chinese themselves understood as Spartan living conditions in order to study in the program.

Figure 4. Beida Library.

Figure 5. The "R" Building.

Chapter 4

Students and Teachers

They sat in orderly rows, both men and women in near-identical olive, navy, or brown trousers and jackets, handwashed and rough dried. It took a very close look to realize that peasant-style Mao jackets were gradually giving way to more citified tailoring. Straight hairstyles still maintained revolutionary decorum while making limited concessions to gender distinction. For older women, the preferred cut was a short bob that covered the ears but did not touch the shoulders; younger ones were permitted pony tails. For males it was a short brush cut, but from their cowlicks and the shaggy fringes crawling about their ears, I guessed that most of them were in the habit of putting off trips to the barber.

In my lecture class on early American history, their daily struggle was to understand and write down everything I said. Pens or pencils scribbling, they hunched over their thin notebooks. No one, it seemed, dared just to listen. When the effort to follow in English was overwhelming, the movement of pen or pencil would stop, and the student would gaze away disheartened. In the first weeks, it was hard to know how much they understood but easy to see the desperation of the effort. When we professors compared notes, we found that most of the questions asked after class were about punctuation, vocabulary, and syntax. They wanted rules of grammar. In vain, it seemed, we urged them to skim over the difficult passages in order to complete homework reading assignments they found impossibly long. At night they toiled away, skimping on sleep, apparently convinced that only a total grasp of each sentence would unlock the key to the next one.

What knowledge in fact did they bring to my classroom? Mr. Ma had told us that they were "Worker-Soldier-Peasant" students who needed better training for their profession as college teachers of English. I knew about this experiment in education under the Cultural Revolution. For two years between 1966 and 1968, most high schools and colleges had been closed down as millions of students, organized into Red Guard battalions, followed Mao Zedong's call to "storm the headquarters" of right wing revisionism in the Party and government. In the summer of 1968, the Maoist leadership put an end to the resulting chaos by dismantling the Red Guards, sending about ten million of them to the countryside to "learn from the workers and peasants" for an indefinite period of time. When schools were reopened in 1970 it was decreed that all students would spend at least two years in the countryside after their terminal middle or high school degrees. The national university examination system was abolished, but universities reopened under new recruitment rules. Following the Party line encouraging "red" over "expert" leadership, the authorities declared that entrance to university would be granted to youth recommended by the humble collectives where they lived and worked. In this way the label "Worker-Soldier-Peasant" student identified a generation shaped by the educational policies of the Cultural Revolution.

When my students in California and I had grappled with this concept, it sounded to us like an affirmative action program for the educationally disadvantaged. But in Beijing something told me that I was not in charge of young people who were being raised above their humble origins as peasant villagers. In fact, it turned out that the vast majority of the students were former sent-down youth—that vast flood of urban teenagers who had been sent to the countryside for re-education. Somehow those in my classes had made their way back to the cities, and to academic institutions which, however crippled, graduated them and were giving them the chance to become university teachers. They had succeeded where less fortunate youth were being left in rural limbo. I also knew that many though by no means all sent-down youth had been caught up in the confrontations between different factions of students calling themselves Red Guards. Were any of my students former Red Guards? I was unlikely to be told and certainly could not ask.

However, there were a few older students who gave the group a more heterogeneous coloration. Perhaps ten were middle-aged women—veteran university teachers of English who had been through the upheavals of the Cultural Revolution and were now being offered something like a mid-career sabbatical. The selection process had also clearly singled out a number from provinces in the interior: Dongbei, (formerly Manchuria), Sichuan, Ningxia, Qinghai, even the far west of Xinjiang. Two—linguistic orphans—had served the revolution as instructors in Russian in the 1950s, and now, aging, redundant, and despondent, were being told to retrain in China's new language of power, English.

I began the fall semester facing this politely silent group twice a week with my lectures on the colonial period in American history. Each lecture class was an hour and a half, and I put written outlines on the board and tried to remember to speak slowly and distinctly. Back in the United States some colleagues in American history had given me advice on basic textbooks and readings, and I had been stimulated by the then-new social history from below that emphasized colonial-era class, racial, and ethnic cleavages. Accordingly I drew on Gary Nash's popular monograph, *Black, White and Red*, and began to highlight the relations of Indian peoples and the white settlers, and the rapid transformations of the social landscape occasioned by slavery. The student response to these themes surprised me.

After about three weeks of waiting alone in the small classroom assigned me for afternoon office hours, I was visited by a group of three young men. They had been following my lectures well enough to offer some criticism. The spokesperson, Xu, was a good-looking, well-built young man with the natural self-confidence that in the United States would have marked a student government leader. "Here in China we are familiar with the Marxist interpretation of American history," he said. "What we want from you is the bourgeois version." Then, to soften the sting, the three began to compliment me on my lectures. "You pronounce all your consonants," they said, and shook their heads over the troubles many had had learning from American Southerners and Australians.

Of course I said there was no one "bourgeois version" of American history, a claim they regarded with polite incomprehension. But in fact this was an "aha" moment for me. I sensed that Xu and his companions were confident that they did not speak simply as individuals, but that their views represented a group consensus. At last I was getting coherent response to my lectures, and one that gave me a real clue about the nature of my audience. Using the Maoist construction which imposed a class identity, progressive or reactionary, on all citizens, I was teaching young "bourgeois

Students and Teachers

intellectuals"! As a native of the advanced industrial and political United States, I was expected to profess the mainstream values of its citizens, and tell the story of American progress uncontaminated by self-critical reflections on American imperfections. I happily switched over from west coast social radical Gary Nash to Harvard University's A-Team—Bernard Bailyn, David Brion Davis, and their colleagues— who had produced *The Great Republic: A History of the American People,* used in hundreds of US classrooms. I did not aspire to creativity. My reference copy of Bailyn was a sturdy pony: enlightenment ideology, the British parliamentary model, constitutionalism, and states' rights. Subsequently my lectures were well received, and as it turned out later, students were able to come up with many critical reflections on American society and history entirely on their own.

Therefore, when Xu together with a second group of students showed up in my office hours in early December, I was prepared to consider that I was receiving some sort of delegation. Moreover, this time the students spoke with a more official voice, because the issue was the public one of Sino-American relations. Was I aware of Washington's recent decision to sell aircraft to Taiwan, the first such sale since Carter normalized relations in early 1979? It did no good to point out to the students that the election of 1980 had brought a more conservative president, Ronald Reagan, into office. Didn't I agree that Taiwan was part of China, and wasn't this sale an affront to Chinese sovereignty and an implicit repudiation of the ground rules of Sino-American friendship? It turned out that all four of us teaching Fulbright professors had been approached on the topic. We realized that a concerted response was needed, so we met and worked out together the language of a public statement we could send to the *New York Times*:

> We see in our daily contacts with the Chinese that this is an issue of sovereignty here, which arouses strong emotions among leaders and people alike.... In Chinese history isolation from the West has much deeper roots than does the tentative internationalism which fosters today's diplomatic and business cooperation, or cultural exchanges like the Fulbright program, now in its third year here. This carelessly arrogant plan to risk the ruin of a rapprochement so painfully achieved is against the long term interests of both countries.

We had achieved the diplomatic language of a press release, and the letter was duly published in the *Times* on January 3, 1982. Perhaps more important for us, our students saw the draft and were satisfied. If other coauthors had any doubts (I was uneasy with the words "carelessly arrogant") they, like me, kept silent. We knew that the credibility of the Fulbright program, and the confidence of our students, was at stake. Struggling daily with the "tentative internationalism" of our own classroom relationships, we had to show by being "friends of China" that they could trust us to be friends to them.

In these early engagements with my students, it was hard to tell where their group impulse to speak out came from. Their request for lectures on "the bourgeois version" of American history had seemed the product of student initiative. The arms sales to Taiwan certainly might have challenged the Beida authorities to justify the presence of American teachers on campus and put pressure on Mr. Ma to encourage a concerted patriotic response. A third controversy that fall was altogether messier. It began with a whispering campaign, escalated to private meetings where third parties heard about matters only indirectly, and eventually drew in our Beida handlers, the Chinese Ministry of Education, and the American Embassy.

It started with rumors that students were dissatisfied with the classes taught by Priscilla Oaks. A product of the academic counterculture of the 1960s, seasoned in the trenches of mass higher education in Southern California, Priscilla prided herself on her interactive classroom. Not only did she insist on building her classes around discussions, she promoted role playing and debates. And her reading assignments featured products of popular culture (magazine ads), the latest countercultural manifestos (*Our Bodies, Ourselves*) or children's books (*The Wizard of Oz*). Murmurs of discontent reached me first through Phebe Chao, who spoke of Oaks with open contempt. Indirectly I was led to understand that Phebe was hearing student complaints and that she also enjoyed the confidence of Mr. Ma about this. Then one day I was summoned to Mr. Ma's office. He looked uncomfortable. What was he to do? Students thought that her classes were not serious. They had visited her but she did not listen. Perhaps I could talk to her?

My subsequent conversation with Priscilla provoked a vigorous defense of her methods. They worked, she said—not only in California but also in China. She had been a great success at her previous year's job at a technical training college in Shanghai. Students had to engage conversationally to learn English, she said. Moreover, in Shanghai students became her friends, and many visited her apartment freely. She even let some of them use her private bathroom, so that they could escape the dismal public bathhouses that served most Shanghai residents. Hearing this I felt somewhat like Mr. Ma. What could I do? I suspected that she was simply closing her ears to real criticisms that were reaching her in the form of indirect language and passive resistance. It seemed to me unwise to try to bully or bulldoze our professionally ambitious Chinese students, who maintained a highly authoritarian model of knowledge production, who were accustomed to the disguises of groupthink, and who were practiced at self-censorship. But Oaks presumably got her present job on the recommendation of her previous supervisors in Shanghai. And interfering with another instructor's classroom violated one of the unwritten rules of American *laissez-faire* academia. After all, I too was a product of the 1960s and the easygoing academic culture of California public higher education.

There was a further issue complicating the situation, I privately felt. As a self-defined students' friend, Priscilla had learned from her class that the Christian Bible and Christian doctrine were totally unfamiliar. Priscilla was resolutely secular herself, but she took it upon herself to address this gap in their cultural knowledge base. Through a philanthropic organization back in the United States she would arrange for Bibles to be mailed to Beida to be donated to all the students in the program. She announced her intentions to her students and they seemed impressed. To get a personal copy of a book, any book beyond the politically correct roster of Marxist authors in state bookstores, was difficult and one of the coveted perquisites of the Fulbright program. No one said out loud that these gifts had to be coming from an American evangelical organization. By November a number of students were asking when the Bibles were coming. When queried, Mr. Ma looked very uncomfortable: he did not know what was happening, he said. But, of course, the Bibles never arrived. None of us thought they simply got lost in the mail. Priscilla was vocal in her complaints about postal inefficiency, intrusive customs inspections, bureaucratic obstruction, and perhaps worse.

By Christmas, Priscilla was in real trouble with the Fulbright program, but the issue was not Bibles, it was that student rebellion was boiling over. Michael and I were called in to a meeting by Phebe, who told us that some students had refused to hand in Priscilla's written assignments and were threatening to boycott any classes she

Students and Teachers   43

offered in the spring. We three remaining Fulbright teachers needed to approve her dismissal.

At this point I was the balky dissenter. The campaign against Priscilla had been conducted in the shadows; we teachers didn't really know who objected to what and why, and Priscilla herself had had no public hearing where she could defend herself. We three were also meeting behind her back and being asked to sign off on a process which would be totally unacceptable in any American academic setting. The case against her had not been demonstrated to my satisfaction. Our meeting broke up without any resolution. Phebe blamed me for the impasse, and I had the feeling that Michael wished the whole imbroglio would just go away.

Then in early January the affair moved to a higher level. Ma called Michael, Phebe, and me into his office. From his point of view, the issue was becoming highly sensitive. Beida authorities had written to the US Embassy, the Chinese Ministry of Education had been informed, and the issue was even threatening to damage Beida's reputation as the campus with the flagship program in English-language development. Though the students were adamant, Priscilla was appointed by the American government, which, Ma implied, gave her official status. So for the Chinese simply to dismiss her was impossible; it even could risk an international incident. Nonetheless, he was asking us to plan spring semester course offerings with three teachers rather than four. The implication was clear: if we did not want her to linger around Beida like an ostracized and disgraced cadre, someone from the American side must take responsibility.

Sure enough, a few days later I was asked to come by the American Embassy and chat with Diane Johnston, the cultural attaché who managed Beida's Fulbright program. She quickly came to the point: problems with Oaks had come to her attention, and did I think Priscilla had been at fault in contributing to the controversy that surrounded her? She did not name her sources or volunteer details, and my reply was also couched in generalities. Priscilla had been stubborn and obtuse, I said. Then I added that I believed she was a poor fit for the Beida program. I knew my words sealed the case against her, and the outcome was a forgone conclusion. The semester drew to a close, students were released to go home for Chinese New Year, and we professors planned winter vacations in warmer parts of Asia. When we returned, Priscilla Oaks was gone, transferred to the Shandong coast to a remote provincial institute of oceanography.

These direct encounters between myself as a teacher and my students were framed by shifts in the larger political winds that occurred over the course of the fall of 1981. The first year after normalization, plus official announcements of Deng Xiaoping's early market reforms as "the four modernizations," had been like uncorking a bottle. A free speech movement called "democracy wall" swept Beijing and other cities in the first half of 1979. People posted "big character posters" on public walls along the capital's Chang'an Boulevard, protesting Party dictatorship and miscarriages of justice. An unemployed worker named Wei Jingsheng became famous for publishing a call for "a fifth modernization"—democracy. By the end of 1979, though, the posters were all torn down, and Wei Jingsheng had gone to jail. What, then, did it mean for Deng Xiaoping's administration to proclaim that there would be "no more campaigns"?

Some hints of an answer came when Community Party Chair Hu Yaobang gave a speech at a grand ceremony staged in the Great Hall of the People in late September 1981, shortly after our teaching assignment began. Nominally the ceremony commemorated the famous revolutionary writer Lu Xun, but there was more. All foreign experts were invited to this event, and foreign experts attached to most

Beijing units were told they were expected to attend. Some foreign experts from out of town were sent to the capital to participate. Hu Yaobang then gave a hard-hitting speech accusing some writers of being "anti-socialist in spirit," "worshipping all things foreign," and forgetting that "art and literature should serve the revolution." The dissident scapegoated in this campaign—for a campaign it certainly was—was the poet Bai Hua. He had authored a film script about a patriotic Chinese artist who returned from abroad to face persecution at home. The title of the film, *Bitter Love,* expressed his love for his country; the film was never shown to the public.

Curiously, we Fulbright professors were not summoned to the Great Hall. Guan told us casually that there was this meeting we could go to if we wanted, but did we want to cancel class? We took the hint and said of course class comes first. Were our cadres trying to protect us? We were after all new in town, and at the very least it would have started our year's assignment off on a dissonant note. The students, we soon learned, did have a political meeting on the topic (they had a political meeting every week). But, one told Phebe, we teachers should not worry because they only had to criticize this one writer! In sum, our Fulbright program operated in a protective bubble supported by our cadres and by the fact that the students were responsible to Beida and not to the home institutions that controlled their futures. Nonetheless throughout the fall and winter our bubble floated in a fog of public rhetoric about the "spiritual pollution" of Western culture. A ripple effect of some sort reached the Friendship Hotel in December when Fred Wakeman, who represented the Committee on Scholarly Communication with the PRC, returned suddenly to California. His wife, Carolyn, clearly unhappy at being left behind with two young children, said that the US government had terminated his position.

I had to feel my own way, alert to hints of boundaries that no one—not me, not the students, or even the authorities—could really name.

In a way, the fall semester had constituted my apprenticeship with my students. It had taught me a new kind of alertness in social relationships—attentive to indirection, to rumor and innuendo among associates whose resources and viewpoints were never openly advertised. I was coming to see my students not only as individuals but as having a corporate identity which could assert itself in surprising ways. But had I seen student power in action, or had I participated in a political theater that was orchestrated by other, higher authorities whose identity remained veiled and whose decisions either took place behind closed doors or were manifest in intimidating public performances pitting orthodoxy against dissent? By the end, what I did know was that I had been disciplined to bend my conduct to the requirements of a "friend of China"—and that my success as a teacher depended upon this. The Worker-Soldier-Peasant students may or may not all have been "bourgeois intellectuals," but they were all in some sense people whose political skills came from the trenches of revolutionary struggles. In this world, I was a novice.

Chapter 5

Student Stories

Bit by bit, a few students began to be more approachable, dropping by the Spartan empty classroom where I held office hours, or even accompanying me for a walk about the campus to get a little extra English practice. Xu Xunfeng, leader of the group that had asked for the "bourgeois version" of American history and a star student in both my small seminars, had broken the ice early on in the fall. He charmed me by paring an apple for me in the Chinese style, carving a single thin spiral of peel with his penknife. A perfect swirl of unbroken skin brought good luck, he said. He also shocked me on a warm autumn afternoon in my office by stripping off his t-shirt and mopping his bare chest as we chatted. But it was a clue that informality was permitted between us, and I found I could ask him questions. When I said that we instructors were curious to know whether any students belonged to the Communist party, he let me know that this was not discussed, even within the student group. I asked him about another puzzling point: why was it that though most were designated Worker-Soldier-Peasant students, I seemed to be teaching young urbanites and not youth born and raised in the countryside? He confirmed my suspicion that most had reached rural areas as educated sent-down youth. His explanation was that the peasants understood that these individuals were more qualified for higher education than their own children, and tended to put them forward for the places assigned under the radical policy of college entrance by grassroots recommendation.

But Xu also hinted how more complex paths of opportunity may have been at work when he explained his own experience growing up in the 1960s. The youngest son of a restaurant manager, he was from Xuzhou, a small town near Nanjing. But his parents had been raised and married in a rural district not far away, and after moving to the city they remained close to their country relatives, sending them money, and visiting often. When the Cultural Revolution disrupted Xu's education, in a burst of youthful idealism he was ready to volunteer to be assigned to a state farm out west. But a report came back from an earlier batch of students sent there that one boy had been so appalled by the barren destination that, weeping, he begged the bus driver to take him home. The driver did not dare do this but told the story on his return. On hearing this, Xu's mother burst into angry tears and threatened suicide if her son was condemned to such a desolate place. The family's old village home was only couple of hours away from Xuzhou, so they arranged for him to be sent to a village where an uncle and others would look after him. There he was soon made bookkeeper for the collective's production team, and after four relatively easy rural years, he was able to return to the city and enter Nanjing University. Mr. Ma told me Xu was considered a rising star in the University's foreign-language division and might even be tapped to join the administration. Almost alone among our group of sixty, he had already been abroad, on a state-sponsored studentship in Canada in 1979. "I was a young leftist and I expected bourgeois decadence," he said to me later, "but I found people who live, love, and work just as we do." It was obvious why he was a class monitor, and my private guess was that among all the students I knew, he was most likely to be a Party member.

If Xu was only one generation removed from the countryside, two of my students told me of childhoods spent in rural communities. Zhao Heping was also a top student, and he had the quiet self-confidence and maturity befitting a young married man whose wife was expecting a baby, and whose job at Hebei University in Baoding, not far from Beijing, allowed him to travel home frequently on weekends. However, he was the child of a coal miner from Yangquan, Shanxi, and when young he worked after school on the village collective farm. Zhao didn't think that his father felt exploited in the mines: the state salary had been good, and he was pleased he had been able to support three children. Zhao Heping was the youngest child and only son, adored by his mother and two older sisters. In secondary school in Shanxi he loved math and music—and played several instruments in the school band; after he graduated in 1973 the music director asked him to stay on and train to be his successor. Later, in 1979, when he had moved on to Baoding and had an offer to study in the United States, his supervisors denied permission on the grounds that he had never really served as a sent-down youth. The Fulbright may have been compensation for this. Talent and a winning, easygoing personality were helping to carry him far from his origins.

The other student who talked openly to me about his peasant upbringing was Zhao Wenxue, a native of Jilin in the far northeast. Zhao's father had some schooling, but the Sino-Japanese war interrupted his prospects and he returned to his native village; by the time Zhao Wenxue, the sixth of seven children, was born in 1951 the family was farming thirteen *mou* (about two acres) and living in a three-generation household. Zhao was the only one of my students who told me a tale of childhood rural misery: "our land got one crop a year; [my parents] were in the fields all day; I had to work gathering firewood and grass to feed the pigs; no one taught me at home. In the winter after you gathered manure and firewood there was nothing to do. My grandparents looked after me; I was my grandfather's favorite, but that was not good." By the time the Cultural Revolution broke out, Zhao was a middle-school student in the county town, and when Red Guard gangs began fighting, "I simply went home and did physical labor for four years." When he entered Jilin University in Changchun, it was his village neighbors who had recommended him. After graduating, he was even sent abroad for a period as a translator, to Zambia, where Chinese engineers had to try to teach local railway workers in English, the only common language.

So it seemed that at least a few of my students were not "bourgeois intellectuals" in the Maoist sense of belonging to elite families, but boys from modest backgrounds who had achieved upward mobility due to Maoist support for basic schooling and the radically egalitarian educational policies of the Cultural Revolution. Besides social class, another category of educational disadvantage was regional, and here the Chinese authorities had seeded our Fulbright program with students from frontier provinces in the far West. I didn't know Huo Hongguang from Ningxia or Feng Xiwu from Xinjiang very well, but Zhang Shengli was one of my favorites. He was a native of Sichuan, but his destination as a sent-down youth turned out to be Qinghai —the high desert plateau flanking Tibet—a vast, sparsely populated borderland far from the centers of Han culture and modern prosperity. When he made it back to the city and higher education it was to Qinghai Teachers' College in the provincial capital Xining, where he would stay. He was a natural pessimist, shy, awkward, and a little grubby, being indifferent to personal appearance. He clearly saw himself as powerless and forced to submit to a life he had not chosen. He devoured the Fulbright program's assigned readings in history and literature with the urgency of a starved imagination, and with talent for the hard questions, speculating from first principles. "Is there an objective social science?" "Do you believe in romantic love?" He dreaded going back home where, he said, there were hardly any books.

If these students had managed to succeed under the adverse conditions of the Cultural Revolution, another student illustrated just how tough the competition was going to be in the future for intellectuals from the Worker Soldier Peasant cohort. Zhu Jinqing was a Beida senior in English literature who hailed from the Jiangnan region, part of the literati cultural heartland in the lower Yangtze valley; he was one of our program auditors. It turned out that he was a member of the famous class of 1977—the first group of young people who gained university entrance by succeeding in the national entrance exams when these resumed after their ten-year suspension during the Cultural Revolution. A decade of pent-up ambition among millions made this the most competitive college entrance examination in PRC history. It was said that only one out of sixty-seven examinees passed.

Zhu had the skinny, almost emaciated body and tapered slender fingers of a traditional literatus; and like the successful examination graduates of imperial China, it was clear he knew he was quicker than almost everyone else. For the first two weeks he wore a little frown in class, letting me know he thought the pace was slow. Gradually he lightened up and admitted to a few leanings of youth, like not wanting the older generation to control marriage. I knew I had passed as a teacher when he stayed after class and wanted to discuss Jonathan Edwards, Thoreau and Emerson—all Puritan utopians—in the light of Mao Zedong thought and the development of socialism. Next he invited me to take a long walk with him around Weiming Lake, where he told me about himself.

He talked about a younger sister back home who suffered from epileptic seizures and how he had studied the classics of traditional Chinese medicine on *tiankuang* madness to find formulas that would treat her. These had been efficacious, he reported proudly, and she had improved greatly. But he was very sad to learn from a recent letter home that she had just died. She had a seizure, fell into a canal, and drowned. Had he still been at home, perhaps his treatments could have prevented this. Zhu may have volunteered all this because he knew I was interested in traditional Chinese medicine, but I suspected that his revelation was also a way of dealing with his guilt over the tragedy in the family he had left behind. As for his English-literature curriculum at Beida, he had been assigned the specialty of Shakespeare studies. This dismayed him at first, but he understood his situation as a kind of arranged marriage. "I felt like a beautiful young concubine who has been given to a strange, ugly old man, but after a while comes to enjoy him," he said. Other students in the seminar kept their distance from Zhu. One later told me he was jealous of Zhu, and he was probably not the only one.

There were twenty women in the program, a third of the total group, and of these about half were older professional teachers, close to my age. All came from educated families, and many had first learned English in the missionary girls' schools that continued to be fashionable among elite urbanites down to the end of the 1950s. My female students were more reticent than the males to speak out in class, but I felt that we related as women. I listened sympathetically to their frequent bitching about sexism in their daily lives, and I was impressed at how often the complaints—about discrimination at work, about the married woman's double burden—sounded familiar. When news got around that I wanted to stay after the end of the Fulbright year to do research on gender and family issues, several were willing to do informal interviews with me.

Zhao Yueying, who was astonishingly lovely, even in her drab clothes, rarely opened her mouth, but this reticence veiled a steely ambition and anger at social injustice. Her girlhood had been scarred by the Cultural Revolution's impact on her father and mother, educated Communist idealists who were severely persecuted as "rightists." She described taking food to them in detention, and watching them frog-marched through the streets with paper labels pinned to their backs. "At a mass meeting, where they criticized and beat my father, I went. I hoped it would help him to see me there. I felt terribly ashamed and humiliated, like I was no good." For two years she and her brother were taken care of by their grandmother. "Ever since," she said, "I haven't trusted people."

Zhao Yueying was very conscious of the career handicaps faced by young intellectuals from the Worker-Soldier-Peasant cohort, and she was determined to overcome them. One day in class the subject turned to abortion and American law, and as a tense hush fell over the group, I couldn't help looking at her and catching a stricken expression. It turned out that she had given birth to male twins just around the time the one-child policy was announced. Her working-class husband and his family were overjoyed at this unexpected good fortune, but there was a quarrel over their desire that she stay home and be a full-time mother. Of her spouse, son of a carpenter and like her a Worker-Soldier-Peasant student, she complained that his family "care for their children materially, but they neglect them spiritually."

Since her own more highly educated parents supported her intellectual ambitions, she took the infant boys to live with them as soon as her maternity leave ended. To Zhao Yueying motherhood was a burden imposed by her old fashioned in-laws, and it was hindering her at work, where "leaders complain about female teachers at our school [that]...when they have children they stop working hard." Though aware that raising her twin boys was hard for her parents, Zhao Yueying was relying on them to help her study in Beijing and perhaps later to help her escape her marriage altogether.

A marriage like Zhao Yueying's—to a social inferior who in a revolutionary society could improve one's political class standing—was not uncommon during the Maoist decades. In some ways, Wu Peihui resembled Zhao Yueying. She described herself as the child of Shanghai intellectuals who was "sent down" to Heilongjiang in the far northeast in 1968. After nine years there she married a local working-class man. She saw her marriage as unusual, but explained it this way: "I was different. I didn't care about marrying a scholar. To me the most important thing was a man's character." She volunteered that for the sake of family harmony she helped with chores in her husband's three-generation household and deferred to her old-fashioned mother-in-law about childrearing matters. When she came to Beijing for her Fulbright year, she chose to leave her young daughter with the Heilongjiang grandparents rather than with her own parents in Shanghai.

If these two young women talked about stresses they faced as educated women in cross-class marriages, a third, Ma Hua, made clear that marriage between elite equals had its own issues. She was elegant, and her clothing was tailored; she worked at the Beijing Foreign Languages Institute and her husband was a diplomat. Early in the fall semester she boldly invited me out to lunch at a new "Western" restaurant that had just opened near the campus, and over an inedible, expensive meal (tough, charred grilled meat we were supposed to eat between slices of bread like a sandwich) I learned her private problem. Her husband expected her to do all the housework and was critical of her cooking. Like many other "bourgeois" city girls, she had learned to do nothing for herself at home, and as a young wife she found the drudgery of cooking began with a daily trip to the market and required all dishes to be prepared from scratch. These confidences may have been designed to excuse her scholastic difficulties, and in making them she looked distressed, frowning slightly. It was clear that she wanted to believe that as long as she was good, charming, and hardworking, life would go well for her. But the Fulbright did not go well, and she soon dropped out of the program.

The older women among my students ranged in age from thirty-eight to the early fifties, but they belonged to an entirely different political generation. The younger cohort had all had their educations interrupted by the Cultural Revolution and its policy of sending all middle and secondary school graduates to the countryside "to learn from the workers and peasants." The older ones had experienced the revolution as young adults in the 1950s, and several had volunteered to serve after graduation by working in the interior—a volunteer program that anticipated the mandatory rustication of young graduates in the 1970s. All were well established in professional careers by the time the Cultural Revolution campaigns favoring "reds" over "experts" argued that education itself was a source of class privilege. I heard from several about how both work and family lives were disrupted, as schools were shut down for two years between 1966 and 1968; between then and the mid-1970s several were sent to the interior or to the countryside for "reeducation through labor." What they wanted to tell me about was how they had coped.

Duan Jingwen had been a young married woman with a teaching job at Southwestern Normal College in her home town of Chongqing when the Cultural Revolution broke out in 1968. She was wondering whether to have a baby. "Nobody worked," she said, lowering her voice, and so "people suggested it was a good time...But I waited for three years. I did lots of things. My husband and I went to the theater and concerts. I had a very good time." After the child, a boy, was born the young couple took turns: "when one was out doing education and labor, the other could be at home." They relied on Duan's parents to care for the child during the two years they were posted away from home, and the household took care of Duan's niece later when her mother, Duan's sister, served in a hardship post in Tibet.

Gong Shaoyu, a matron in her forties, was clearly content with her marriage to a fellow professor at Zhongshan University in the far south city of Guangzhou. She too had given birth to a single son around the time the Cultural Revolution broke out. When the boy was fifteen months old, he was sent to live with his paternal aunt, who lived nearby, was married to a working-class man, and had several children of her own. This arrangement supported Gong's career and provided a home for the child when Gong and her husband were "sent down." Like Duan, Gong offered few details of her political rustication, and commented only that she had had to take over as a parent when the child was seven and old enough to study. "He sometimes calls their place 'home,'" she said. "He says our place is 'school.'"

Under these circumstances, it is not surprising that Gong defended the traditional multigenerational family, which was helping her, like my other women students, manage the rigors of their lives in revolutionary society. Once she bragged to me that, unlike American boys, her now fifteen-year-old son would bring his future wife to live with them and "stay with me all my life." At the same time she was proud to belong to the generation that had benefited directly from the Maoist policies of education and employment opportunities enabling women to "hold up half the sky." So comfortable was she with the contradictions of gender ideology in her life that perhaps I should not have been astonished by her contribution to a class discussion of gender difference. Males are naturally more intelligent than females, she said. When I sputtered a protest, asking her about the performance of boys and girls in school, she reaffirmed her conviction. "Once they become adolescents, girls fall behind. It's biological." The other students in the class did not challenge this version of mid-twentieth-century science education that Maoist propaganda had not effaced.

If these two older women glossed over their harsher experiences as intellectuals in Maoist China, they also seemed willing to leave them behind. Two other older women had sadder stories with more tragic consequences. Their problems had begun earlier, in 1957, when the original "anti-rightist campaign" to enforce Maoist orthodoxy was sweeping the country. In a panicky response to a short episode of encouraging criticism of the Party—"letting a hundred flowers bloom"—the authorities cracked down on intellectuals who spoke out. Sun Dalai was from Shanghai, but she had graduated from Beida in the early 1950s and had married a fellow Beida graduate from an elite family. Of her mother-in-law Sun said, "she was like a woman of your Old South," unable to adjust to revolutionary society. Sun's husband was sent to the interior, to Shanxi, in the late 1950s as a result of the "anti-rightist" movement. Because of his "political difficulties" and their prolonged separation, they had only one child, and in the early years of his exile she had returned to Shanghai to live with her parents and to raise her daughter with them. In the late 1960s, as they realized he would probably never get permission to return to Beijing, she went out to Shanxi to join him. When I met her in the Fulbright program she was forty-eight years old, teaching at the

Shanghai Institute of Foreign Trade, and widowed. Another student told me her husband had committed suicide.

But what Sun Dalai wanted to talk about was her now twenty-four-year-old daughter, who lived with Sun and her parents in Shanghai. As a toddler, the girl had been diagnosed as mentally retarded. This child was raised by her Shanghai grandparents, who lovingly sheltered her, and ironically, the Cultural Revolution helped her graduate from middle school. "There were no exams and no studying was expected," Sun explained. Further, "a middle-school graduate must be placed [in a job] by the municipal authorities...so when that was about to happen I got leave from Taiyuan [in Shanxi] and came home to talk to them. Because I was a native of Shanghai who counted as having 'gone to the interior' to serve society, my case got priority and was listened to." Sun's daughter ended up in a steady a job on the assembly line at a lamp factory located not far from their apartment. "Everything has two sides," Sun reflected to me. "Our system is hard on clever people and doesn't let them show their talent. But for someone slow like her it provides for them well." Sun's major worry was about what would happen when her parents were no longer there to provide a home, and she was curious about social service alternatives to family care in the United States.

However, the saddest story came from a tall, gaunt woman with wide-spaced, somewhat protruding eyes. Gu Yiting was a Beijing native, gently educated at one of the missionary schools for girls in the capital. At the age of nineteen she had gone to work for the foreign-language division of Beijing radio and had married a man who was an announcer there. When the "anti-rightist" campaign broke out in 1957, and every unit had a quota of "rightists" to identify, she was a natural candidate for the political enemies list. Her transgression: "I made some criticisms of the 'back door.'" Exiled to the far north for almost two decades, her life was essentially ruined. She and her family lived in an incredibly poor village, where the exiles were forbidden to read books. The local peasants were good people, she said, but when they asked her to tell their children stories from traditional romances she was afraid that to do so would invite more criticism. At the nadir, she was separated from her two daughters, who were taught to reject her. Now officially rehabilitated, she was back at Beijing radio, where she worked side by side with colleagues who had originally denounced her. Offered this year of study as a kind of reparations, she knew it was too late. When she "spoke bitterness" to me she used the idioms of the currently popular "scar literature" that allowed victims of Cultural Revolution excesses to tell their stories. But I felt she spoke less to condemn the Communist regime than to explain her profound depression that no books or teachers could now ease.

By the end of the fall semester two women attached to the program had become my friends. To my surprise and delight Li Shuyan and Fan Lanying did not seem to be constrained by the official disapproval that surrounded fraternization between us "foreign experts" and our students. It took some time to figure out why.

Li Shuyan caught my attention early on in the large lecture class I gave on American history. Short, slight, with iron-grey hair cut in the standard short bob that Maoist convention decreed for older married women, she sat in a front row, following closely and with apparent ease. It turned out she was a professor of English literature at Beijing Normal University, and close to my own age. Moreover, she lived just across the street from the Friendship Hotel, in an apartment complex reserved for employees of the Chinese Academy of Agricultural Sciences, where her husband worked as a scientist. Imagine my delight when she invited me for dinner! I passed the gatekeepers of her unit without challenge, traversed the shabby garden courtyard, and walked up to a second-floor two-bedroom apartment where she lived with her husband and two teenage daughters. The living/dining room was strewn with books, newspapers, and documents to be read. Her cooking was practical—stir-fried dishes that could be produced with little fuss. It all reminded me of the way women intellectuals in the United States juggled domestic and professional lives. At family dinner she was at home and in charge. Her husband, wearing carpet slippers, dined and shuffled off, friendly but taciturn (he knew no English); after eating, her daughters were under discipline to return to their desks and grind through mountains of school homework. What did we talk about? She wanted to know about literary studies in the United States. She had written about Jack London—a safe American author for Chinese in the PRC—but she was interested in Faulkner, in Asian American literature, and in the new postmodern literary theories that were popular in the United States. We didn't talk Chinese politics or about the Fulbright program itself.

Gradually I learned a little about her family background and her career. Her father had been a Nationalist general, but when he decamped for Taiwan in 1949, he left her mother and their three children behind. Another, more favored woman (wife? concubine?) went with him into exile. Li Shuyan won a place at Beida in the early1950s, and in 1958, shortly after she graduated, she volunteered to go to the interior as a teacher. "I was a revolutionary in my youth," she explained. Out west, in Gansu, she met and married her husband, who belonged to the Chinese diaspora in Japan, but who had come back to the motherland to help build the New China. The couple kept their precious Beijing registration, helped by Li's mother who took care of their daughters in Beijing until the parents could be reassigned to live and work in the capital. Of course none of this protected them during the height of the Cultural Revolution, but the family were survivors, skilled at steering within the boundaries of the permissible.

Concerning that traumatic episode, Li's most specific complaint was about its effect on her daughters. After finally establishing themselves as a nuclear family in Beijing, Li and her husband were separately "sent down." Summoned to leave immediately for work in a steel mill in far away Lanzhou, she had to leave her two girls with a neighbor. She was gone for two years. She felt that her relationship with Li Chun, the older child who had already entered grammar school, survived the separation. But as Li Chun now prepared for college, her mother reflected sadly, "I only had her for seven years." As for Li Min, the younger girl, "she loves her nurse."

So we both had teenage daughters and hopes for their educational progress, but where I was casually optimistic ("Bella will get into college; everything will be fine"), she was tense with anxiety. She taught me about the "narrow gate" into nationally ranked public universities. If you suspected your child's college entrance exam scores were going to be on the low side, you steered her toward a major that was less crowded and a university that was less competitive. College students and their families did not like to move out of their home dialect area, whereas the state wanted their young talent to circulate nationally. Li Shuyan had determined that Li Chun should prepare to be a chemistry major and apply to Xiamen University in Fujian province, far to the southeast. If Li Chun had reservations about this plan, she largely kept them to herself. In any case, the state educational authorities would have the last say about placement, major, and broader life chances.

If university was not enough of a challenge, unlike me Li Shuyan saw her daughters' marriages as a maternal responsibility as well. Marriage prospects for highly educated young women were poor, she explained, largely because the Cultural Revolution had caused so many men to drop out, or to join the military, reducing the pool of suitable mates for daughters of the intelligentsia. At the same time, a Chinese woman who stayed single would be socially marginalized, seen as odd, or the object of scandalous rumors. Li was already busy canvassing the field for daughters of her friends, where a further source of frustration was that choosy young women rejected candidates too easily. As for freedom of marriage for the young, she explained that young people were expected to look for mates who had been vetted by their families, but now they had veto power.

Li Shuyan could more easily reach out to me as a friend because she was a senior scholar who lived and worked independently from Beida or the Fulbright program. Fan Lanying, in contrast, was young and served as Mr. Ma's part-time assistant. She had been a Fulbright student in the previous year's program, taught by experts in English as a second language (ESL). Early on, Fan sailed into the Friendship Hotel, apparently secure that she was authorized to be there with messages from the program director. There were few entertainments available in Beijing in 1981. Public restaurants, bars or nightclub were almost nonexistent, and tickets to the few state-approved theater or musical performances were doled out through an opaque party patronage system that I never understood. Several times over the course of the fall, she appeared at my door on Saturday morning with news that we had tickets to see Beijing opera that night. Ma, it turned out, was a great fan and was thrilled at the return to the stage of a renowned company attached to the PLA.

And so my friendship with Fan began at the opera, where she sat next to me and translated plot points as I was introduced to several classical dramas and to performances by the last surviving male artists who specialized in female roles (*dan*). These frail actors found conveying an illusion of femininity no challenge, but they had a hard time overcoming their now-advanced age. Fan, by contrast, was full of the vitality of youth, with a softly rounded oval face, sparkling dark eyes, and hair done up in pony tails (standard for young unmarried women) that danced to her animated talk. She was twenty-eight, almost past the age that orthodox opinion decreed proper for a Chinese woman to marry. Commenting on this, she speculated that she might well never marry. But Fan seemed happy with her independent life, her good job as English teacher at a local technical college, and the residence permit that allowed her to live in her native Beijing after years of being a sent-down youth in Inner Mongolia. Fan was available for Chinese lessons, excursions, and girl talk, including gossip about the previous year's Fulbright program and about our Beida supervisors.

Watching Fan and Ma chat happily during the intermissions of our Beijing opera excursions, it was clear to me that our Fulbright director and his young assistant had a warm relationship. She could form a friendship with me because he approved of it. In fragments of personal history, Fan communicated to me over several months, Mr. Ma figured as an important mentor. His patronage had helped her to leave Inner Mongolia to join the previous year's Fulbright program—the authorities had wanted a Mongolian native, but when no one could be found with enough basic English to qualify, they were persuaded to let her serve instead. When she finished the program, he recommended her for her teaching job. If she was grateful to him for all of his help, I laughingly suggested I should be grateful too. "He sees I am alone here and he has assigned you to be my Chinese friend." She laughed too. "It is fine to have an official friend; you just have to be careful that it is someone you would want as a friend in any case."

Over time, I learned a good deal about her personal history. She was the youngest of eight children. Her father had been a self-made capitalist, who rose from youthful poverty to become the owner of several dye-making factories. Until the Cultural Revolution, the family had prospered: they lived well and all the children were well educated. But ironically, his business success, once praised, was now condemned. The Fans had become "bourgeois capitalists." Red Guards from her elite private school had invaded the family house while her parents were away, trashing the piano and books, breaking all the phonograph records, and forcing her to eat coarse grain while they scarfed down the household stock of good food. "They told me I was a teachers' pet," she said.

Political persecution had driven her parents from their comfortable home to a tiny makeshift shack in Beijing, but Fan didn't offer details about this or the exact travails suffered by her siblings. About her years as a sent down youth in Inner Mongolia, she chose to sound upbeat. It had been hard to go months in the cold without bathing, but she had learned to ride a horse! The steppe, rich with midsummer pasturage, was spectacular. Her host family were wonderful people with whom she still kept in touch. And anyway in the end her language skills were a ticket back to the city—to the Inner Mongolian capital of Hohhot, which needed staff for their English-language radio program.

By the time I became Fan's friend, her parents and siblings were all reunited in Beijing, beneficiaries of the new state program offering restitution to victims whose homes and property had been confiscated. I was invited to meet many of them crowded into Fan's tiny apartment for a family party. They had survived, they were together, and to hear them tell it, they hoped to be successful again.

Stories like these came from the students who sought me out, but their narratives left out a good deal. I heard only a little about revolutionary activism among the older students, and no one among the younger ones identified themselves as having been militant Red Guards in the late 1960s. If they were careful to downplay their more troubled experiences, I interpreted this as part of a collective desire to put the past behind them. This showed up in the way everyone navigated the Marxist social class identities which had played such a key political role since 1950. My half-ironical label of them as "bourgeois intellectuals" unraveled as I learned of lives that moved between city and countryside, of multigenerational kinship networks that crossed social boundaries, and of upward as well as downward mobility. In distinguishing between themselves and the "working class," my students firmly identified themselves as people who worked with their minds rather than their hands. They were intelligentsia (*zhishifenzi*) who had studied hard and whose talents had been recognized. Marxist class categories were only labels; the social distinctions of culture and learning that really mattered to them were as old as Mencius.

Were my students simply the lucky ones, who had managed to navigate the shoals of the three Maoist decades and had gotten safely to the post-Mao shore? For an American arriving in 1981 the novelty was to see middle-aged veterans of the first revolutionary generation rededicate themselves to their careers, and especially to hear some upbeat stories from young adults ready to consider their tumultuous adolescence experiences something that taught them to better understand their country. Over the year, this appreciation was reinforced, but I also came to see how the dark side of the previous decades cast a long shadow.

Figure 6. With students at the Beida Library (Winter 1981).

CHAPTER 6

AMERICAN STUDIES

In reintroducing the Fulbright program into China, the diplomats at the American embassy in Beijing were ambitious for the exchange to break new ground in Sino-American cultural understanding. Where at the beginning of normalization in 1979 the Chinese authorities asked that we send them English-language teachers, the Americans wanted to place experts in "American Studies" programs, with interdisciplinary focus on history, society, and culture. Our Foreign Service was following a pattern of subsidized "American Studies" programs that had been successfully introduced into a number of European universities beginning in the 1950s. (American Studies also developed as an interdisciplinary undergraduate major on many American campuses.) But in 1979 and 1980 the very idea of American Studies was unfamiliar to China's educational authorities, and Americans remained locked out of most Chinese universities. Our program bringing advanced students from other universities to Beida was a hybrid experiment. With advanced language immersion as our basic assignment, we teachers didn't worry about defining American

Studies. We all taught composition. Michael Yetman and Phebe Chao did American literature. Assigned a history lecture course and a broad social science seminar, I seemed to be in charge of everything else.

My lecture course, meeting two mornings a week, addressed all sixty students in the program. I knew how to introduce comparisons between China and the United States into my lectures—reversing descriptions I had used back in California. Ecological comparisons: Manchuria is like Maine; the Yangzi delta is like the American Southeast (could have been a rice bowl!); the far west of China resembles Utah and Nevada (they ride horses out there!); parts of Yunnan are like New Mexico, complete with eroded sandstone mesas and petroglyphs. Demographic comparisons bring out differences: the incredible contrast between the lightly settled colonies and the intensively cultivated fields of late imperial China; sociological contrasts: why neither pre- nor post-Columbian America had anything really comparable to the historical peasant population of rural China.

I also introduced into my lectures some standard themes that Chinese historians of my generation ruminated over. Joseph Needham, much admired in China, provided evidence of the imperial empire's technological sophistication as well as an argument about why there had been no "scientific revolution" in seventeenth-century China. John Fairbank, dean of the study of Ming–Qing China's foreign relations, emphasized the imperial state's indifference to overseas trade, using as example the fifteenth-century voyages commanded by the imperial admiral Zheng He, who took a large fleet as far as the east coast of Africa before the court discontinued support. Scholars of my generation all contrasted this with the commercially driven maritime explorations of the Portuguese and Dutch. I did not try to refine these observations to take into account revisionist views that American historians of China were beginning to entertain in the 1980s. It was enough just to touch on topics that reflected commonplace beliefs about the comparability of East and West—to put China in the frame of a class on American Studies, so to speak.

In my efforts to follow the pattern of an American college lecture course as closely as possible, I had touted the pedagogical virtues of an essay-style final examination. Somewhat doubtful, students did accept that they would simply be asked to come into class and to write out their prepared answers to two or three questions selected from a study guide handed out in advance. Their answers to the exam showed that in spite of their professed interest in "bourgeois" history, most of them were more comfortable thinking of issues in early American history in terms of class conflict. They thought that the rivalry between Federalists led by Alexander Hamilton and anti-Federalists led by Thomas Jefferson pitted the rich, who were northerners and merchants, against the poor southern agrarian farmers. Jefferson puzzled them (doesn't he still puzzle us all?). They were not accustomed to think of private property as a foundation of the republican social contract. How could Jefferson be a champion of the poor farmers and common people and at same time assume that these people would defer to the landed elites as their rulers? How could he be both a radical republican and a slave-owning plantation master? At the same time, they decided that Hamiltonians were afraid of the common people and did not believe in the doctrine of natural human goodness. (Students all followed Mencius and Voltaire in professing this optimistic view of human nature.) Students who identified democracy with direct rule by the people (though not necessarily with ballot box expression of this) had a hard time getting their heads around the electoral ideal of representative democracy or the federalist structure of states' rights.

As for the American Revolution itself, one common view was that it was a national liberation struggle against an oppressive colonial domination. They were quick to assume that nationalism formed the basis for a republican consensus in the new nation. Concerning the American Civil War, they kept to economic interpretations of history —it was a struggle between capitalism, represented by the manufacturing and entrepreneurial north, and southern agrarianism. Yet, they were in no doubt that the unionists were the good guys because slavery was obviously evil; they didn't see any of the abolitionists as extremists. But it was harder for them to see the way race prejudice against African Americans overrode sectional differences, making poor non-slave-owning southerners support the Confederacy and delaying Republican embrace of emancipation. In sum, they interpreted the Civil War through the paired lenses of political economy and morality play.

Like lecture courses on history in the United States, this one involved passive learning and few public questions. In the end, it seemed that the views of Bernard Bailyn and his Harvard colleagues had made little impression on the class. Reading over their exam essays, I felt they had hewed pretty close to the interpretations that would be found in PRC state-approved textbooks. Perhaps some students had used these as their own pony. At least their English composition skills had improved.

However, American Studies broadly speaking included far more than history lectures. We were exposing them to a whole range of novelties: fiction, art, theater, social commentary, and—perhaps most thrilling—movies, many of which were provided by the embassy from lists we teachers supplied. The students' more spontaneous responses did not emerge from the large lecture class, but bit by bit in the small seminars where, for two afternoons a week, my group of fifteen to twenty were assigned topics and readings for composition and for the seminar dedicated to American society and politics. Gradually they became accustomed to submitting unsigned written questions for me to answer. They produced these on the tissue-thin sheets of note paper that were the commonplace student stationery of the time and, like nineteenth-century letter writers in America, they covered every inch of surface with writing, wasting little space on margins. If the text did not fill a complete page, they would tear off the written fragment and save the rest. Over time, they began to ask questions that were not based on the day's assignment. Though they never clamored to speak, on most days I could expect a few volunteered verbal comments before the class ended. I had heard from Priscilla Oaks that the previous year some of her advanced students in Shanghai had asked permission to rewrite papers on Freudianism, afraid these might find their way into some official dossier or other. With this caution in mind, I made a practice of returning all signed writings to the authors.

An early experience that was fodder for class discussion was a travelling art exhibit of American paintings from the Boston Museum of Fine Arts. The Chinese authorities had fretted over the fact that the Boston curators insisted on including a dozen abstract paintings in the exhibit ("decadent bourgeois art"). But they need not have worried. The students were respectful when Phebe Chao offered a brilliant tour of the collection, but what they liked best were the nineteenth-century genre canvasses of landscapes, cowboys, and Indians. Looking at an abstraction they found disguised figurative images, much as Chinese traditionally have interpreted rock formations and mountain ranges; a few conceded that calligraphy embodied an abstract aesthetic, though connecting this to Jackson Pollack was difficult.

When their literary readings came up for discussion I found that they were impressed at how Americans can say "no." They read

Melville's "Bartleby the Scrivener," in which the hero's reply to every situation is, "I would prefer not to." However, where I had always understood this as the tale of an unhappy asocial recluse, they were impressed by an individual's bold claim of a right to be left alone. John Updike's short story "A&P" for me evoked images of antique beauty in three girls who visit a seaside convenience store in their bathing suits. But something stopped the students short: was it possible that the protagonist, a teenaged clerk, could respond by just up and quitting his job? What Americans read as a modern evocation of a bewitching classical pastoral of three graces, the Chinese students saw as an almost unbelievable flouting of permissible behavior. The kid was off to the beach, but he would certainly live to regret this!

Why did Americans like literary realism, they asked, when stories of ordinary everyday life are depressing and boring? When they read Willa Cather's "Paul's Case," most had no sympathy with the hero's suicide; he should have stayed honest and worked hard. That is how you get ahead. A similar strand of moral didacticism inflected their responses to a number of films (screened privately, of course, and outside regular class hours). Seeing *The Glass Menagerie*, they refused to identify with the shy daughter (though many of them struggled with painful shyness themselves.) They thought Jim, the "gentleman caller," was the model character, and that everybody should be more like him. As for *A Streetcar Named Desire*, Blanche DuBois was simply a dissolute woman. Their interpretations may not have been as insensitive as these responses suggest. It is as if they had learned it was too threatening to allow yourself to admit failure or to identify publicly with life's losers.

However, this was not the end of the story. They wanted film (like Chinese opera) to take them to a fairy tale world of romance, and Hollywood understood: everyone loved *The King and I* and *The Sound of Music.* Nonetheless, their absolute favorite film was *One Flew Over the Cuckoo's Nest.* Through their eyes, I suddenly recognized the mental hospital as a socialist madhouse, structured around arbitrary daily rules and psychobabble group speak, and presided over by a sadistic mommy-nurse. The inmates, lobotomized by this regime, are stirred to anarchic and hilarious rebellion by a manic newcomer (Jack Nicholson) who creates a "great uproar under heaven!" like the Monkey King of the famous Buddhist fairytale. Of course the inmates can't win, but who is really crazy here? I should have known: Milos Forman, fresh refugee from Communist Czechoslovakia, had found his subject in Ken Kesey's beat fable.

No one confessed to being interested in religion as a spiritual practice, but the curiosity surrounding Christianity was tinged with a sense of fascination with a taboo. On one level, like secular citizens of late twentieth-century America, they were ignorant of the Biblical references that stud much classic American fiction, and they were relieved to learn that English majors at Harvard (like my son) also needed to bone up on the Bible as literature. But their fascination and bewilderment went deeper. As Xu Xunfeng said to me after class one day, "How can it be that the people of an advanced industrial civilization like the United States continue to believe in these superstitious stories?" Questions began with the obvious: What is all this about Adam and Eve? Who were David and Goliath? How is the Old Testament different from the New Testament? Finally Michael Yetman and I agreed to hold a special lecture class on the story of the Bible, and over two hours a fascinated throng listened as he ran through a complete narrative from the Fall to the Atonement, while I supplied occasional commentary. I was even able to recite the Twenty-third Psalm that I had learned in Episcopal Sunday school. Public response to all of this afterwards was both guarded and tactful, but a couple of students did say that the life of Jesus made a passionate and compelling story. They knew about the martyrdom that could befall fighters for social justice. As for Priscilla's imprudent offer of a Bible to every student, nobody was going to turn down a free book.

The reading and writing assignments about American society and politics included a formidable roster of works on political and legal thought. Thinking that students also needed something readable on American social life, I picked *Middletown: A Study of Contemporary American Culture* by Robert Staughton Lynd and Helen Lynd. This classic social science case study of Muncie, Indiana, in 1929 described a small-town America that in many respects continued to feel familiar fifty years later. At a basic level, there were plenty of unfamiliar social facts to explore. What is a chain store, what is a sorority? The installment plan? A "petting party"? Moving up the ladder of complexity, what is anthropology, the census, a weighted average? Protestantism? Secularism?

But even more so, by combining quantitative field surveys with the narrative focus of an American leftist, this book satisfied the students' assumption that "objective social science" would reveal class relations and class conflict in action. Forgetting about their interest in "the bourgeois version," they revealed their belief in the rise of rationalism and science as a tide of history leading to working-class emancipation and socialism. The book showed that class contradictions in America have been sharp, just as they had been told. But why, one asked, was there no resistance? The portrait of public education in Muncie showed that schooling failed to equalize. From the cradle, working-class children had different experiences and more limited opportunity. Didn't the victims of exploitation want to revolt? "Where was radical consciousness?", one asked.

As for the consumer society criticized by the Lynds, the idea that the economic well-being of the group depended upon an appeal to people's most primitive acquisitive instincts appalled another student, and most were not swayed by the idea that mass consumption creates jobs.

However, the theme of competition and career success resonated with the students. We were drawn into conversation about competitive "key schools" in China. Some were prompted to wonder whether heredity or environment determine destiny—or rather how one can really know about this. Others were willing to admit that material comforts have value, and that compared to Chinese most people in Muncie led comfortable lives. Not for the first time I wondered if the quickest to speak up in my discussion sessions were those who articulated politically correct left-wing opinions. Doubts were more tentative, and opened the door to questions for which the nascent post-Mao world had no answers, any more than I did. How can a consumer society be a socialist one? How can competition lead to equality? No one was sure.

At first everybody seemed to be on the same page when they responded to the portrait of private life in Middletown. All those divorces must be signs of family breakdown. The emancipation of women is good because it allows them to move into the work force and earn money. China is progressive about this, while American complacency about broken homes is truly decadent. Even though I knew privately that several students had unhappy marriages, no one would defend divorce as an institution. And although the Lynds talked about conformity, the students thought small-town life in Muncie was a riot of individualistic hedonism. Matrons may have been economically dependent upon their husbands, but they enjoyed club life and social engagements. As for the young, what about all those "petting parties" and running around in cars? Didn't American students ever worry about their studies? But when I asked whether their sympathies were mostly with the young or with their parents, they were firmly on the side of the students, and some expressed skepticism about the long-term viability of the Chinese joint family system.

However, their ambivalence about how to think about American society was demonstrated again when I assigned them to write short papers on such topics as "Middletown's women: are they emancipated?" or "Social classes in Middletown: harmony or conflict?" Some panicked. Wouldn't I explain "the American point of view?" I could see that they liked the safe haven of that phrase, and I was goading them to actually choose between an orthodox Marxist interpretation and one of their own devising. Of course I could not push them too far here. Not surprisingly their formal essays on such set topics tended to be relentlessly bland, in contrast to the occasional sparks that lit up classroom verbal exchange.

For a more contemporary look at social problems, they read Michael Harrington's *The Other America*, which produced a barrage of questions about poverty. I tried to satisfy their demand for figures, challenged by their skeptical questions about the statistics involved: "what is an urban minimum standard?", "How about regional variations?" Clearly the data supplied involved a "numbers game" but what was it, exactly? They listened politely to my explanations that Great Society programs of the 1960s like Medicare had helped the elderly but left children, African Americans, and the unemployed behind, and to my account of debates between liberals who traced poverty to race prejudice and economic hardship and conservatives who harped on culture and individual responsibility. But the overall response of most was shock at the persistence of poverty in a rich country and at apparent public complacency in the face of it. They took easily to the language of social welfare: there should be subsidies and pensions to deal with this.

Then we moved on to an intimidating collection of political documents—Locke and Hobbes, Thomas Paine, the Declaration of Independence, the Constitution, and the Federalist Papers. The students had Bernard Bailyn's *The Ideological Origins of the American Revolution* to guide them through these thickets. I would go over the readings in class and then ask them to show in a short writing assignment something of what they had learned. They could tell me that the British constitution was not a written document but a collection of laws and precedents that guided practice, that the American constitution was based on the social contract theory of John Locke, that in early modern Europe governments were organized into estates to represent different social groups, and that this gave rise to the idea of representative government in America. And so it went. It was useful language practice, and they were after all good at learning stuff.

Throughout the fall of 1981, in fact, the official Chinese press was full of articles about constitutions and constitutional revision. It was pretty clear that the new Communist Party leadership under Deng Xiaoping was preparing the way to revise the current constitutional document—the one produced by the Maoists in 1975 at the height of the Cultural Revolution. The new version would be the fourth constitution promulgated by the Chinese Communist Party since 1949. It was interesting to speculate on how the language used by Party "framers," which labeled constitutional documents as "models" and seemed to understand them as bureaucratic policy directives, conveyed aspiration rather than founding doctrine. As I followed these news reports I wondered whether the students were aware of them too (did they even read the *People's Daily*?) but I knew better than to suggest US–China constitutional comparisons as a basis for class discussion.

In my own mind, the American Constitution's staying power did have something to do with the fact that it grapples with the machinery of political and legal decision making as well as policy ideals. But I had only limited success in getting my students to appreciate the workings of the federal system of government and the balance of powers between legislative, executive and judicial branches. Responding to *The Federalist Papers*, one student was vocally unconvinced that a purely political organization of government according to the principle of "separation of powers" could possibly be effective in balancing competing agendas, which he thought had to be understood as based on class interests. Madison simply did not understand that "some interests are more powerful than others," he said.

Further, they did not seem particularly impressed by the American constitutional organization of electoral politics, either its federal political structure or its electoral machinery balancing the two houses of Congress and the executive. They remained not only children of the Chinese Communist revolution, with its class-based understandings of political power, but also citizen-subjects of a centuries-old polity where centralized authority was simply a given, seen as inevitable. However, when I went over the articles of the Declaration of Independence, the room went quiet with the sort of alert attentiveness a group gives when they want to grasp every word. Hands went up to ask about the meaning of eighteenth-century language: "establishment of religion," "unreasonable search and seizures," "grand jury." In this room there were people who knew first hand what it was to experience authority's knock on the door, arbitrary searches, interrogation, prison, exile, or even the threat of death. In Jefferson's text, the social contract had the authority of moral commandment.

Accordingly, their essays took on life when they were asked about "natural rights." Everyone agreed human beings were born with some things they were entitled to: "freedom of efforts to strive for a better life," "rights to live, work, study, and enjoy." Or they quoted John Dickinson: "rights to guard himself against any encroachment upon personal liberty and property.... cannot be taken away by any human power without taking their life." These rights "born with us... cannot be taken from us."

When I tried a question about whether governments are necessary in order for people to live together in harmony, I got strongly statist views. Groups need a leader as a human body needs a head, to protect the people from disruption and suffering; without government "the weak are bullied by the strong," and one could expect "chaos and anarchy." One bold student used as an example "the recent Cultural Revolution," when "all governments were dismantled, all authorities except Mao were despised, and all rules were ignored. Social values were shaking, there existed no lasting sense of right and wrong, production couldn't continue smoothly, people couldn't maintain their personal security and private property."

Some other students speculated that the New World environment of colonial America may have fostered rural communities blessed by natural abundance and out of the reach of state power. One student projected such an Arcadian alternative onto a utopian communist future: "when communism becomes true, governments together with classes and parties are no longer necessary...and all people in the world are a community in which people are equal, there are no oppression and exploitation, people will live harmoniously as brothers and will strive together for still a better life."

In my students' voices, I could hear their own experience and their instinctive rather than memorized responses to the history we labored to study. And it seemed to me that some of their understanding of the doctrines of human rights could be linked to Chinese socialist readings of the Enlightenment, which had been popular among early twentieth century reformers like Liang Qichao. I wondered whether they connected the vision of a future without government to the ancient utopian ideals of "Great Unity" as reconfigured by the great late Qing reformer Kang Youwei. But I didn't probe to find out whether these names of early Republican reformers long sidelined by Communist doctrine and policy meant anything to them. It did seem as though the tension between their optimistic accounts of human nature and their fear of anarchy without strong government had been inherited like cultural DNA from the ancient political theories of the Confucianists and the Legalists—doctrines they were unlikely to have acquired through any formal exposure to classical or reform thought, but which would have continued to inhabit the mores of family and community life even in the Maoist era.

We discussed the American income tax. I had procured copies of the 1040 form. Reasonably enough they wanted to calculate the actual average taxes paid by people at each income level, not the theoretical rates. They entered gleefully into speculations about how Americans figured out how to game the system. What about withholding done by automatic deductions from pay checks. Was that fair? It was clear that this showed that on one hand life in the United States could be complicated, but on the other hand they were fully equal to the challenge of figuring out how to maximize advantage. Everyone knew that capitalism is about profit, not virtue.

Their study of American elections was stimulated by reading Theodore White's *The Making of the President 1960.* Just like the income tax, elections are a way to understand the nitty-gritty of the American political system. What leads to a candidate's nomination in the first place? Why don't Americans just have a national primary and be done with it? Of course behind all of this political theatre is the power of money. Several wondered why Rockefeller wasn't automatically a candidate in 1960 because he was obviously the richest. There was naïve populism—in a democracy ordinary people ought to be able to rise to the top—side by side with the most hard-bitten cynicism.

It was amazing how quickly they concluded that understanding politics is a matter of unmasking behind the scenes manipulations. We discussed Supreme Court rulings supporting *laissez-faire* economics and one student commented that of course all the Supreme Court justices must be businessmen. Their tactical questions about the arcana of democratic politics—the processes underlying primaries, caucuses, selection of delegations to nominating conventions, and the role of media and polling as well as money—exposed my own relatively simplistic understandings of these things. I complimented them, saying tactfully that an outsider's perspective was often acute. One agreed, "of course outsiders see more clearly." But when I asked whether I as an outsider might understand China better than the Chinese, he looked shocked.

In hindsight, who understood politics best? I, certainly, believed that their being confined by Maoist official media would lead to the kind of reflexive distrust that gives almost any backstairs rumor potency. But was I, perhaps, not as sensitive as I should be to the subtler boundaries that keep our American mainstream free press inside a comfort zone that discourages radical criticism?

In response to student requests, I prepared short special lectures on equal rights under the law, the rights of defendants in criminal trials, anticommunism in American life, the Great Society social programs, and money in politics. The 1960s, and the presidencies of John F.

Kennedy and Richard Nixon, were particularly fascinating, perhaps simply because these were within the living memory of most of them, but also because they showed American politics in action in situations that were filled with conflict and drama.

I could see students were wondering whether nominating conventions such as we had in 1960 and 1968 explained the dynamics behind a seemingly open political party process. If policy platforms drawn up by special party platform committees were dismissed as insignificant, as many American pundits said, why have them? Shouldn't members of a party share basic views on the issues? Moreover, wasn't it dangerous for members of the same political party to attack one another in public on the floor of the convention hall: surely their opponents would take advantage of this later? It would seem that party conventions were no longer controlled by bosses such as were described in their American history textbooks, but then who was in charge? Was it worth while to have televised debates between the candidates if the popular response was shaped by personalities and image rather than issues? From all this, I gathered that for many of them the cacophony of American political competition shocked their sense of the decorum that should surround any sound political deliberation. Finally, the tumult drowned out what was basically at stake: Please, Professor Furth, will you explain to us the exact difference between Democrats and Republicans? (I gave standard "New Deal" answers, only half aware of how rapidly these were becoming obsolete.)

The topic of presidential powers was another favorite. First of all, there was the question of whether an ordinary person "from the broad masses" could actually become president. They had heard stories of humble beginnings about many, but weren't all the candidates already public leaders? (I tried to give them a sense of alternative career paths by tracing the family histories of the Kennedys and the Nixons.) Money, especially the contributions of big donors, was clearly important: were the donors personal friends of the president, and did they expect to be repaid? Did the president enjoy financial and tax privileges? Behind all these ruminations about the perquisites of office was a deeper question about presidential power itself. These powers, vast to begin with, were presently increasing, they thought, and as one astute student noticed, control of the nuclear button made the vulnerability of citizens especially clear. If the Constitution was based on the doctrine that a president's power is limited, how could congress and the people tell when a president oversteps the boundaries? Would they know, and could they do anything if they did? (In my role as defender of America's liberal traditions, I tried to remind them of the constitutional checks and balances, but I couldn't help being impressed with their intuitions that an "imperial presidency" had evolved in the Cold War era.)

All of these issues came into play as the students dove into the sensational topic of Watergate and Nixon's resignation from office. The Watergate scandal had begun to consume American politics in the spring of 1973, just about a year after Nixon's famous February 1972 visit to China, which ended over twenty years of her diplomatic isolation from the "free world." Nixon, therefore, was already celebrated in China as committed to improving Sino-American relations, and students recalled that the Chinese official media were pretty muted about his troubles back home. One student had seen more detailed accounts in *Reference News*—the internal press for party members and cadres—but "the pity was I didn't follow it closely." In class, our guide to these events was *The Role of the Supreme Court in American Government* by Archibald Cox, the constitutional lawyer who in May 1973 had been appointed by the US Senate as special prosecutor in charge of investigating the Watergate burglary. When Nixon rejected a court order to turn over White House tapes of conversations relevant to the burglary, it was Cox who insisted that the president comply with the rule of law. Nixon had Cox fired by the Attorney General's office in October 1973, but when the Supreme Court upheld the court order in August 1974, it was clear the President had to resign.

For most students, the starting point was sympathy for Nixon, who as president had shown himself to be such an effective friend of China. His resignation was unfortunate, they felt, but as one put it, it "saved his face." Some even thought that a factor in the case was opposition to his China policy, and submerged here was concern whether the policy of opening to China was imperiled by his departure. Others believed that his conduct was not particularly praiseworthy, but suspected that dirty politics could be found on all sides of the affair. He had powerful enemies—"monopoly interests" perhaps, or "industrial or sectional interests." The machinery of government was dominated by his political adversaries, the Democrats, who used the case to bring him down. Others in American politics had operated in similar ways, but he had the misfortune to get caught. His aides were stupid and gave him bad advice, or worse, some were disloyal and "betrayed" him.

Remarks like these showed that Watergate confirmed most students' instinct that all politics is a raw contest for power involving factions of rival loyalists whose members do not state their aims out in the open. So it was not surprising that many struggled to understand what exactly what crime Nixon was guilty of. What he did "was considered illegal"; "he had broken American law"; "it was factually unconstitutional for a president to engage in such conduct"; Nixon's White House aides had "committed crimes and done something unconstitutional." With guarded phrases like these, they made clear that they thought more was hidden here than a White House conspiracy to protect Nixon from investigation. Moreover, although they accepted the American people's outrage at the spectacle of official corruption, they did not see much difference between ordinary criminal transgression and conduct that was unconstitutional.

What many did see, on the other hand, was that Watergate showed how a president's power could be challenged successfully. The doctrine of the separation of powers, studied previously as a constitutional abstraction, appeared in muscular practice, and its muscle seemed to reside in the Supreme Court. They were not particularly struck by the role of Congressional committees or acts of impeachment. It was the Supreme Court that could condemn his deeds as unconstitutional. Nixon broke the law, and "the Supreme Court found him guilty." If, as one student commentator put it, Watergate shows that no one of the three branches is supreme, another praised the court as a "checking machine" above the other two branches, and a third defined it as "supervising" them.

Alone of American political institutions, the Supreme Court—as evoked by Archibald Cox—gripped the students' imagination as the institutional embodiment of American republican virtue. It seemed to demonstrate the principle that no one is above the law. Defining what law is was more difficult: there was the distinction between an unlawful action (like burglary) and an unconstitutional one (like relying upon a flawed interpretation of constitutional law itself, as in the case of Nixon's appeal to "executive privilege" to sequester White House documents). There was also the issue of constitutional interpretation as it has been practiced over the course of American history. Here several student admirers of Cox's portrait of the Supreme Court were deeply disturbed as they came to realize that Cox portrayed the Constitution as evolving, continually reshaped by case-based court decisions that involved judgments about new circumstances. They were particularly shocked by Cox's example of how the laws punishing libel had gradually weakened through Supreme Court decisions in cases involving press freedoms. Press freedom was abstract to them, but "slander" was a weapon of personal destruction they took very seriously. In sum, their foundationalism was instinctively Biblical: law should stand as a set of principles of justice recognized as immutable.

Although I tried not to steer discussion in provocative directions, I could not help suspecting that many students did not think American and Chinese historical experience differed fundamentally. We shared some Enlightenment assumptions: that human beings are naturally good, that government should serve the people's welfare. They responded positively to the American Declaration of Independence, and to the Bill of Rights, while remaining skeptical of the machinery that governs on a daily basis: whether political organizations or the machinery of electoral politics. Law was an abstract ideal unmoored from institutional guardians. The press was less a "fourth estate" than a complex and untrustworthy kaleidoscope of propaganda and entertainment. There was plenty of evidence that Americans had engaged in armed struggle (the American Revolution, the Civil War), in the repression of dissent (the civil rights and labor movements), and in cutthroat factional contests for power (the impeachment of Richard Nixon). Should I not have been surprised when one bright and sophisticated student was ready to claim that the Cultural Revolution in China had been more moderate than our American mid-century struggle for racial justice?

This left me wondering what their overall picture of the traumas of the Cultural Revolution might be. I knew they had followed the shifting campaigns in the official press and that they had struggled to make sense of its ideological implications. Several had said to me they had given credence to party directives for several years, giving up only when the chairman's designated successor, Lin Biao, suddenly fell from power in 1971 and they were told he died in a plane crash while fleeing to the Soviet Union. They also all had individual stories —and those I heard about testified to a wide variety of experiences. Among the older generation some had devoted their youth to the ideals of the revolution, while intellectuals condemned as "rightists" suffered most. Among my group of Worker-Soldier-Peasant students, the experience of being "sent down" varied, depending on their personal networks as well as luck and talent, making generalization difficult. But beyond the individual level, the only collective story publically available in China in 1982 was the obviously unsatisfactory trial of the Gang of Four, condemning extremists but protecting Mao personally and with him the Communist Party.

We Americans celebrated freedom, but, ironically, the younger students' most immediate experience of personal freedom had been the Cultural Revolution itself, when people seemed to go wild. "Everyone was crazy," as Fan said. The examples of American freedom that bubbled up from our classes on literature and popular culture were seductive, but in their celebration of individual desire and gratification, were they not also dangerous? My students were unanimous in their longing for more choice and less interference in their private and professional lives, but our year-long seminar in American Studies did not seem to offer guidance for them to connect these private wishes to a reformed public order.

Chapter 7

The Visiting Professor

Air travel from North America to Asia today is not radically different from what it was in 1981. A jet airplane carries its load of passengers and luggage across the Pacific in from twelve to fourteen hours. But virtual communication has been radically transformed in the intervening thirty-five years. When Monty and Bella said goodbye to me at the Los Angeles airport in late August 1981, we knew it would be difficult to talk on the telephone from China and that we would have to rely on letters. Unsure that even an electric typewriter could be reliably used and serviced in Beijing, I decided to bring an older manual machine whose accessories—carbon ribbons, ink whiteout, carbon paper, and even mimeograph paper—were still easy to find in the United States. Using this equipment I would communicate with home via typed letters.

To telephone Los Angeles from Beijing required major logistics. First it was important to set a day and time in an exchange of letters in advance; then, while my husband waited at home, I would have to make my way downtown to Beijing's Central Post and

Telecommunications Office, stand in a long line until I could be assigned an open phone cubicle and an operator who would dial the call. Naturally under these conditions our conversations were brief, practical, and conducted in the sort of strained elevated voices that I recall my grandmother using for long-distance phone communication in my childhood in the 1940s.

With letters we were thrown back to the venerable traditions of epistolary relationships, not so different from those our Victorian ancestors used to craft themselves in the process of revealing their lives to others. Letters suited me perfectly: once or twice a week I transcribed into words the daily flood of impressions, giving them the stability of a text in the manner of field notes or a diary. Some guests at the Friendship Hotel had stories about intercepted mail and worried about political surveillance by the authorities, but I refused to be inhibited, preferring to imagine that my mundane scribblings were too insignificant to attract notice. My only strategy was to make carbons of everything and send these back in batches with American travelers flying home: a precaution that turned out to be unnecessary. From my letters, Monty could see exactly how absorbing my life in Beijing was, and his letters assured me that back home familiar rhythms continued, and particularly that our daughter was surviving high school without me.

But letters did not always paper over the vacancies created by separation. This may have been the age of airmail, but we soon found that we shared a problem that Chinese friends in America had told me about: if you waited until a letter arrived from across the Pacific before responding, it could seem as if weeks passed with no news. If you wrote spontaneously and often, letters crossed in the air, and miscommunication resulted. Monty and I found that although his letters to me arrived in four or five days, mine to him took at least twice as long, and sometimes several appeared in his Los Angeles mailbox in a bunch. He wasn't hearing from me as often as he would like, and when they arrived, my letters were all about the new experiences I was having every day. Monty wrote that he felt my letters were too impersonal, that they were fascinating but lacked intimacy. I knew what he was thinking: they revealed that I didn't really miss him; I didn't want to be home.

And this was entirely true—if my vocation as a historian was to explore China, the Fulbright year was more than the long-delayed opportunity afforded by a political opening. After twenty-five years of marriage and two children, I was finally set loose on my own to pursue a lifelong dream free of domestic chores or family obligations. The Friendship Hotel, that segregated gilded ghetto for foreigners, cocooned me from responsibility for daily living arrangements, and outside its gates the historic city and its citizens, and a whole nation, were available to explore. The barriers of culture, language, and politics that made access difficult and understanding elusive just made the entire enterprise more absorbing. Monty had his own solution to the psychological vacancy he felt. He would join me. He could easily take a quarter's leave from his teaching job, we would travel during the winter break surrounding the Chinese New Year, and then he would spend two months with me in Beijing. How could I object to this? It would be wonderful to have him as a companion during the month of January when all of us Fulbright professors turned into tourists on holiday. Beyond that I could not begrudge him an interlude when he too would be exposed to academic life at Beida, and I would learn how my relationships in China might appear in a new light when I resumed my normal identity as a married woman. Certainly my students seemed to take this to heart. At the end of the fall semester, on the eve of the holiday, a group braved the guarded portals of the Hotel campus to pay me a visit, crowding into my apartment living room, beaming, and presented me with a painted scroll of "mandarin ducks"—symbols of marital felicity.

Monty duly arrived on January 8, 1982. In the airport, still separated by the customs area's plate glass window, we joked about our "conjugal visit." Even apart from our personal reunion, the trip—his first to Asia—was thrilling for him. Soon he was writing amusing letters home about the immigration bureaucracy, the denizens of the Friendship Hotel, the "bloody cold" weather, the adventures of bike riding in Beijing, or of experiencing socialist-themed Chinese movies in the Hotel through earphones that offered mangled English translations of the dialogue. There followed a month of intensive travel and sightseeing. First was a VIP tour of southwestern China in January organized for the Fulbright team by our Beida supervisors, who enabled us to bypass the cumbersome bureaucracy that in those years deterred all but the most determined independent travelers.

Provided with documents permitting us to visit a half-dozen cities and with a full set of train or air tickets between them, we did not have to apply for permission to move on at each stage of our trip, stand in long lines in freezing train or bus stations to get tickets, and just hope that the local hotel for foreign guests would have room when we arrived. In several cities (Chengdu, Kunming, Guangzhou) we were hosted by students in our Beida program who were home for the holidays (older scholars, reasonably well established at local universities). We rode the amazing then-new pioneer rail lines that run north–south through the mountains from Xian to Chengdu in Sichuan, and then on to Kunming in Yunnan (Monty kept track of the number of tunnels, which ran in the hundreds). We made an overnight trip to the temples on the Daoist mountain Qingchengshan and suffered a fortunately brief bout of food poisoning from the monastic

The Visiting Professor

evening meal (not vegetarian, alas). We gaped at the towering Loshan Buddha, took a day hike on the lower reaches of Emei mountain, renowned as a Buddhist pilgrim destination, and retreated to our Kunming hotel room as the local citizens celebrated the new year with twelve hours of fireworks that approached the intensity of an artillery barrage.

We had a wonderful time!

Back in Beijing, my teaching duties resumed, but the weeks were punctuated with trips to all the major tourist destinations in and around the city, plus a full menu of the cultural activities organized by the Friendship Hotel for its residents. In the fall I had declined to participate in much of this as I worked to keep one class ahead of my students, but now I went along as these activities supplied Monty with an exposure to the local scene far richer than that available to the normal tourist.

More interesting to me personally were a succession of activities the Beijing authorities staged for the edification of the capital's foreign community. One was a conference and exhibition commemorating the tenth anniversary of the death of Edgar Snow, American author of *Red Star over China*. This journalistic coup reported on Snow's journey to Yan'an, the Communist revolutionary base camp in the far northwest just after it was established in 1936. Snow's book introduced the English-speaking world to Mao Zedong on the eve of World War II when he was still only a radical guerilla leader in the hills of Shaanxi province. Snow, because of his support of the Communist-led war effort against fascism and of the infant PRC after 1949, had been forced into exile in Switzerland in the 1950s. Now in 1982 in Beijing hundreds of Chinese and Westerners turned out for speakers who included Snow's second wife and widow, Lois Wheeler Snow, and Huang Hua, China's first ambassador to the UN and current foreign minister, whom Snow had befriended on his famed trip to Yan'an in 1936. Monty and I both noticed Huang Hua's fervor, as he spoke of Snow as the man whose book made Mao Zedong known to the world, and (in Chinese translation) to his own compatriots as well. Snow, then, was revered as a participant in the Chinese revolution, not just a sympathetic journalistic observer of it, and a portion of his ashes lay on the Beida campus under a commemorative tablet overlooking Weiming Lake. Monty and I passed it several times on strolls about campus, and we also caught the message that Snow represented a standard for "friends of China" today that we Americans should take to heart, in light of the tensions over Taiwan that were surfacing in these early days of normalized relations.

On another occasion we were invited to sit in on a criminal trial, this time an event designed to educate the foreign community about China's post-Mao policy of respect for the "rule of law." Several hundred of us foreigners sat with earphones in a large municipal court auditorium to witness the case brought against a man named Li Yunfang, accused of embezzlement. Monty saw right away that this was in no way a trial as we in America understand it: the defendant's guilt was assumed. He had worked for a state railway company which needed to expropriate property for a proposed right of way, and he had cheated the citizens of the compensation due for their displaced houses, pigpens, latrines, gravesites, etc. (a case like this could not have involved land, which was not privately owned.) If there had been witnesses deposed, this had happened long beforehand. In laying out the evidence of Li's guilt, the prosecutors were establishing a record of their investigation and its conclusions, and demonstrating that their proceedings had been proper, orderly, and judicially dignified. Asked at intervals if he agreed with the narrative as stated, the defendant always said yes.

If anything was still at issue in this unfolding legal morality play, it was the degree of culpability that fit this particular crime. Someone who seemed to approximate a public defender made a plea for leniency by noting that none of the embezzled money was "splurged" and that unspent funds had been returned. In his own defense Li chimed in that he had "financial difficulties"—to care for a sick wife, dependent children, and other relatives; he needed money for grain, and to repair and rebuild his house. The judge rebutted this sternly by saying that the basic issue was not the amount of money involved but the breach of public trust. The ideological root of the problem could only be solved if the guilty man reformed his political outlook. After a twenty-minute recess, the judges returned and pronounced a sentence of three years in prison.

As he was led away after the sentencing, Monty and I both thought that the defendant was smiling. Perhaps, we concluded, he knew that he would be rewarded in some way for agreeing to play the role of public scapegoat so obediently. As Monty speculated, what had occurred behind the scenes may have resembled a plea bargain. Certainly Li's issues fit in with concurrent political media campaigns about the economic crimes of corrupt officials. (We had seen a *China Daily* article, "Hundreds Confess to Smuggling.") Later, reading over Monty's detailed family letter about the proceedings, I realized more clearly that this "show trial" closely followed the formula used in late imperial case law: a formal record of a trial would be submitted to higher judicial authorities to justify the conclusions reached. The resulting "appellate" review process most often involved adjustment of "severity" or "leniency" of the punishment in light of culturally orthodox understandings of the gravity of the offense. Communist rectitude did not look that different from the Confucian version.

Monty was more than a privileged tourist, however. He was also a "visiting professor"—a published philosopher from a well-known American university. The Beida philosophy department had heard about him. Introductions were made through He Zhaowu, a professor of early modern European philosophy at the Academy of Social Sciences. Professor He had been educated during World War II at Southwestern University in Nationalist-controlled Yunnan, but had spent his career at the Academy unable publicly to pursue his interests in Pascal, Rousseau, and Kant. Monty and I had met him briefly in 1979 on He's short trip to California—an official gesture toward his rehabilitation after hardships we could only imagine. Now He was to help Monty reach out to philosophers in Beijing. An awkwardly jovial restaurant dinner followed, leading to an invitation to give a series of lectures—at Beida, and perhaps also at the Academy of Social Sciences. Monty suggested the topic of "origins of ancient Greek philosophy," thinking to draw upon his introductory UCLA lecture course on the pre-Socratics. Good. Intellectuals in China were very interested to learn more about the origins of Western science, we were told.

Excruciating negotiations followed. The chair and vice chair of the department who visited us at the Hotel were ready to schedule lectures on Heraclitus, Parmenides, and Empedocles respectively to be delivered one week apart beginning on March 5. But arrangements broke down over the question of a translator. I was ready to propose one of my better students. But would these be familiar with philosophical terminology, they asked? Wouldn't it be better for the translator to be from their own ranks? Monty was agreeable—he was agreeable to everything—and it was arranged that he would prepare a draft and that Mr. Li Deqi from the department would come to the Friendship Hotel where they would go over it together two days in advance.

Mr. Li duly turned up, accompanied by a colleague, and in a state of terror. "I am not prepared," he said. He had been given the assignment only twenty-four hours before our meeting. Sweating profusely in spite of the cold room, he reluctantly accepted Monty's proffered draft text, promised to return to discuss it the following day, and fled. But the next day it was the chair and vice chair who turned up again. Mr. Li was sick, they said. The lecture would have to be postponed a week. Once again we raised the possibility that one of the Fulbright students would do, and suggested Zhu Jinqing. They will look into it, they said. In the end Monty went to the university still unsure who if anyone would translate, and found that Mr. Li, now recovered, was on the task. In carrying out his translator's assignment, Li paid no attention to any text, but stared at Monty's face and launched into extensive remarks that sounded like improvised commentary and extended the whole performance to almost two hours.

After the end of this session, some backstage discussion must have occurred; we later learned that for a Beida or other student to play a formal role in a unit to which he was not assigned required permission from higher authorities. Even the cultural affairs officer at the US embassy heard about it. Somehow, for lecture number two Monty was paired with Zhu Jinqing , and they managed a competent joint effort. For the third lecture Li returned to the stage, by which time he and Monty were more attuned. Monty had learned to produce very short sentences, and Li's Chinese version, though ridiculed by Phebe Zhao, did not leave the Sinophone philosophers in the audience looking as though they needed to go to the bathroom.

I confess that I have totally forgotten the content of any of these strained efforts at Sino-Western intellectual exchange. We knew from informal conversations that Beida philosophy students were complaining that their one course in "Western philosophy" consisted of potted accounts of "schools of thought" with ready-made Marxist interpretations. I knew just enough of the classical "one hundred schools of thought" of China's ancient "Warring States" period to see the futility of trying to frame the history of Western philosophy this way. Someone tempted to connect ancient Chinese thought with ancient Greek counterparts would face challenges far beyond the abilities of any of us. For Monty it was an interesting, somewhat exotic exercise he could toss off, like a bottle containing a message, into a wide sea and leave it to its fate. For the Beida philosophers, marooned on their island of Marxist-Leninist theory, there was a touch of desperation in their effort to climb aboard the ship of Western learning my husband navigated with apparent ease. To save face, Li had to translate; as "friends of China" we had to pretend that our communication had been profitable. The event was recorded, and Monty left behind transcripts of his lectures. If anyone ever retrieved them from the dust of philosophy department storage, we never heard of it.

Shortly before Monty left China, Professor He Zhaowu invited us to a restaurant dinner with his wife—a gesture of appreciation that was the clearer for being indirectly expressed. Professor He gave us a copy of his Chinese translation of Pascal's *Pensées*, now available, but he was too dignified to expose more than a hint of the privations and disappointments of his career. He wore his rumpled Mao suit and PLA-style cap with the mild severity of a socialist puritan. A rule of socialist table manners dictated that one always leave room for a plain bowl of rice at the end of a banquet meal. We had done so, and when his wife carefully piled the leftovers into a tin box she produced from her handbag, we received a lesson in socialist frugality and also one about the financial costs that hosting a restaurant meal imposed on people like them. He Zhaowu left me with the impression that he understood exactly why our exchange on Greek philosophy and the origins of science was so limited, and also why such exchanges were necessary.

However delightfully our days together had passed, the season of the visiting professor felt more and more like a vacation from my primary mission. With my husband as constant companion, out of deference to him almost all my interactions with Chinese took place in English. Fan Lanying stopped coming over to practice with me; the momentum toward greater Mandarin fluency, always halting, slackened. The Friendship Hotel itself, cocooning its cosmopolitan Western residents with in-house services and a round of entertainments, seemed more and more like a ghettoized resort. Among foreign residents who had left families behind, the long late winter, with endlessly grey and sooty skies, took its toll on relationships. One friend fantasized obsessively that her lover back in Berkeley was unfaithful. Another quarreled with a spouse who came for the winter holiday and who reacted to the alien environment with rage: it was for *this* that you broke up the family for a whole year? What were you thinking? Luckily for my marriage, Monty's visit had the opposite effect: as a visiting professor, he shared my China world for the first time, and this ignited in him a sympathy and interest that allowed us both to be more relaxed about the months of separation that remained.

Nonetheless, as he flew home in late March, I felt restless. The rumor mill at the Friendship Hotel buzzed with stories of official efforts to limit Chinese contact with foreigners. It was said that Party directives to this end were being studied at the unit level. More about "spiritual pollution" was being hammered in the press. Someone said that cassettes of western music had all disappeared from a downtown shop that had formerly sold them. Yet at the same time, there were signs of a glacial shift toward more open relations in the scholarly community. Beida was about to open a campus residence hall for foreign graduate students and visiting academics; next year's Fulbright scholars would be living on campus, and would be assigned to university programs as was normal in other parts of the world. I dreamed that perhaps I could jump start a greater immersion in Chinese life by moving there for the remainder of the academic year.

Ma promised to try, but he looked worried. "Are you sure you want to do this?", he asked. "It will not be very convenient"—the classic evasion that left open the question, inconvenient for whom? Maybe I should look at the accommodations first. When young Zhou took me around one Sunday soon after this conversation, it was clear that the case was doubtful. Beida's foreign affairs office had not yet gotten authorization. Maybe the rooms would be needed for visitors from Berkeley. Fan confirmed my sense that I was an object of suspicion. In the fall I had participated in a Beida panel discussion organized by students on campus about women's liberation in the United States. At the time I had shrugged it off as a failure: eighty percent of the student audience was male, and, perhaps to cover their embarrassment, they had mostly asked snarky questions about American divorce. But, Fan said, "the authorities know everything." They knew that I had a long-term scholarly agenda, and people thought that I wanted "to talk to women," she said.

Hearing this, I wanted to push harder, but Ma was simply unavailable. It was now a familiar bind: in a world where information was filtered through rumor or communicated by indirection, I could choose between paranoid speculation and hopeful common sense. After all, the new dorm had only eight rooms ready for use; Ma had done his best to help me, and to protest further only trapped him between the authorities he served and the Fulbright clients he was assigned to satisfy. I was learning to negotiate social relationships by holding back, by monitoring myself to keep others out of trouble.

So it was settled that I stay in the Friendship Hotel. Three more months to go.

Figure 7. With Monty at the Forbidden City (February 1982).

Chapter 8

Spring Fever

Spring in China is the season of outbreaks, and officially spring begins early, right after the lunar New Year. Ascending *qi*, stimulated by the lengthening days, encourages the stored "Cold Damage" of winter to become active, and prudent people know that this is a time to be moderate in exertion and to take tonics against Wind and Damp. Spring is socially contagious as well. Long before June Fourth (1989) there had been the anti-imperialist protests of the May Fourth (1919) and the May Thirtieth (1925) movements. For centuries the Qingming (Spring Brightness) festival of the spring equinox was a time to remember the dead, and if possible go on an outing to sweep ancestral graves. As recently as April 5, 1976, protesters had gathered in Tiananmen Square, claiming the right to mourn the death of Zhou Enlai and in so doing to register their opposition to the policies of the Gang of Four. Few of my students could have been participants in this, nor could they practice ancestral rituals—which were still disapproved by the authorities anyway—but they began to be restless.

Tired of the cramped dormitory barracks they lived in, fed up with bad food, they were also getting tired of work.

After Chinese New Year it was still bleak and windy, but Beijing residents began to say that the worst of the winter had passed. In the apartments along the road to Haidian, on the balconies that residents used as winter storage, the piles of cabbages that had stacked up since October visibly dwindled, and in the Friendship Hotel dining room we were served precious fresh vegetables—cucumbers, radishes, even tomatoes—grown under the plastic cold frames that were just beginning to be used by farmers in the suburbs. Gradually we could ease up on the layers of long underwear, boots, hats, and padded down jackets that had been necessary in the previous months, and the bike ride to school became almost pleasurable.

And flu season came to the Friendship Hotel. Overcome with fever, sweats, and diarrhea, I took to my bed, which provided another occasion on which a group of students came to the hotel campus to visit me. Damp with perspiration, limbs limp and wrapped in untidy sheets, I was too prostrated to do more than wonder dimly what view of social etiquette could make anyone think that this was the proper time to come to call. But visiting the sick was clearly an approved form of Chinese sociability. Crowding around my bed, they explained the seasonality of illness: according to the twenty-four divisions of the solar year, a person will be able to feel a change in the weather every two weeks, and after the New Year has passed, the rising *qi* of the seasons of "light rain" (*yushui*) and of "insects stirring from hibernation" (*jingzhi*) stimulates pathogens along with other forms of natural life. They brought Chinese medicine—a prepared formula in the form of round walnut-sized balls the color of mud and with the aroma of medicinal earth—to be dissolved in hot water and taken as a sort of tea: a febrifuge to judge by the results. Luckily they did not offer the purgatives often recommended for seasonal "Damage from Cold" in traditional medicine.

Other hotel residents were also experimenting with remedies recommended by their Chinese coworkers. Luckily for me, one American acquaintance had fallen ill much earlier in the season than I had. After three weeks during which Chinese medicine had failed to improve her lingering diarrhea and fatigue, she had gone to a biomedical doctor attached to the French embassy. He had identified the spring pathogen as the parasite *Giardia*, and had prescribed the amoebicide Flagyl. Deciding that Western bodies were not well adapted to Chinese remedies, I followed her example, and for the sum of US$30—substantial in the local economy—got diagnosed and prescribed for at the French embassy compound. The doctor must have been making very good private use of his hard-currency earnings, for his waiting room was filled with elegant Ming-Qing porcelains (floral motifs in delicate green and rose on a white background) such as I had seen in museums but in no local shops.

By the end of March, what I could recognize as a real spring had arrived. The spindly trees in the courtyards of the Friendship Hotel all turned out to have blossoms—crab-apple, cherry, quince, and others unknown. The sticklike bushes along the median of the highway adjacent to the compound turned out to be lilacs. Along with the flowers, fresh winds made the air feel spring-like. But instead of rain, we experienced a spring dust storm. It advertised itself as rain would: the sky turned sallow, yellow-grey, the air stilled as it does when a front moves in, and then it "rained" dust, which came from high up and had blown in from far away. Blinding, gritty, it made every one flee for shelter. Fail to do so and dust sculpted your facial lines, invaded your undergarments, and coated your teeth. Afterwards the sky cleared and fresh winds blew, just like after a rainstorm, while at the Hotel the drain waters from compound sinks and showers soon ran brown. But I wondered about the absence of "April showers." Does this famous windblown silt that has fertilized the North China plain for centuries take their place? It finally rained on April 24, the first time since I arrived eight months earlier.

Full-blown, blooming spring did lighten the mood of my students along with the weight of the garments we all wore. I gave a party at the Hotel and everyone from my seminar came—they wanted beer and chocolate cake! Beer was every day, but a chocolate cake cost twenty yuan, half a month's pay for many. In class, my seminar students were more relaxed, and discussion was less stilted. I continued the practice of soliciting questions on unsigned slips of paper, but their spontaneous follow up comments were more free.

Class discussion tended more towards the personal. I learned that American feminist images of how "women hold up half the sky" did not fit my students' views of the matter. A number of women students had used the assignment "Write an essay using example as an expository device" to complain bitterly about the job discrimination they had encountered in the work place, and the assumption that as wives and mothers they were responsible for the family at home. In one case, a woman said she was forbidden by her husband to employ someone to clean house on the grounds that this violated socialist morality! Another complained that in her unit, an aeronautical institute, the grants to English teachers to study abroad were for men only. On the flip side, a couple of male students opined that women's liberation may have "gone too far" and one even contrasted the serene world of his old-fashioned mother with the harried one of his intellectual wife.

If Maoist ideology had not succeeded in inculcating socialist gender equality, it had left sexual issues embedded in an ambiguous conflation of political and personal morality. This emerged when we discussed the recent American movies that the embassy was beginning to supply to us as well as to other academic units. The selection of films reflected an American cultural diplomacy that aimed to highlight progressive social ideals. But my students responded most strongly to the personal themes. It was easiest to understand their response to *Kramer vs. Kramer*, in which a divorcing couple's custody dispute focused on a stay-at home wife who abandoned the family, claiming a need for independence, and a workaholic husband who had to learn to care for their small son. Because American norms (in which custody goes to the mother) were simply reversed in China, where it was assumed that the father (i.e. the paternal line) keeps the children, a story of the bonds formed through a father's active care of his son seemed entirely natural to them. Instead they focused on the fraught topic of divorce itself, as unseemly and harmful to the family. As the instigator of the separation, Meryl Streep was simply a "bad woman." But in another film the "bad woman" turned out to be Sally Field's *Norma Rae*, in the biopic about a woman union leader organizing North Carolina textile workers. One explained: How could a woman who was the mother of an illegitimate child and the mistress of a married man be a good political spokesperson for the group? Didn't the union leaders object?

If all this revealed the tenacity of traditional norms about gender and kinship, their response to another film really surprised me. *Julia* depicts an American woman writer's gradual political engagement in the anti-Fascist movement through her love for her childhood friend, Julia, who had become part of the underground resistance in 1930s Germany. The students did not comment on the existential European struggle against Hitler, or on the submerged theme that socialist progressives needed to join the fight. "What," they asked, "is the relationship between Julia and Lillian [the heroine]?" They assumed they were seeing a lesbian romance.

I was fascinated to try and find out what cinematic signals suggested to them the erotic interpretation of a film most people in America, myself included, had chosen to read as a depiction of the sisterhood of two independent women fighting for justice. Well, they said, Julia is strong like a man, and Lillian admires her as a woman would a man. She seems to love Julia more than she does her husband. They hold hands, they dance, Lillian says, "I love you." All of this led some also to question whether a woman like Julia could be a model revolutionary heroine.

If Maoist art set the standards, the bar for moral rectitude in revolutionary leaders seemed impossibly high. But what about life? This led to the question how my students defined "pure" versus "impure" love in same-sex as well as heterosexual situations. I asked them to fill out a simple form evaluating the moral weight of (1) erotic fantasies, (2) intimate language and gestures like kissing and handholding, and (3) clinical sex acts, among same-sex and opposite-sex couples. The tabulated result of this anonymous survey, which I put on the blackboard, suggested that few Chinese revolutionaries would make the grade as "pure." Most students were in theory strongly committed to severe self-monitoring of erotic fantasies of any kind. But they were far less strict about erotic acts, and if I guessed that my class included a several highly inhibited individuals, a healthy minority were not, including a few who were tolerant of same-sex desires. After class, a couple of male students explained to me privately that guys could play around if they didn't go too far. "Males can get away with things because no one expects male friendship to be impure," one said.

Further surprising contrasts in our sexual cultures were brought home to me another spring day when Li Shuyan and I went by ourselves to see a special visiting exhibition of *ancien régime* paintings from the Louvre. If the French authorities wanted to show the Chinese that they understood pre-revolutionary decadence, they succeeded. Having been habituated to Beijing's visual culture of revolutionary sobriety, what I saw was a frenzy of Baroque excess: dynamic, exhibitionistic, sensual canvasses, openly catering to a male taste for erotic titillation. They all seemed to depict crypto-Greco/Old Testament fantasies of rape, abduction, or torture in which writhing bodies clustered around some archaic hero or saint. Everyone seemed to be gesticulating wildly, clothing in disarray or half falling off, males with rippling bare torsos, females entirely nude or with a coy breast or two in tempting flesh tones peeking out here and there. Then there was Louis XIII looking like a pouting halfwit, all decked out in Arcadian costume with a wreath on his fat head, surrounded by blowsy nymphs. Only David's portrait of the assassination of Marat stood out clean as a knife blade, with marvelous echoes of a Renaissance pièta.

Poor Li Shuyan didn't know where to look. She kept gazing at her shoes; from time to time she lifted her head and asked in stifled tones, "and what is the story?" about some "Rape of Europa" or "Abduction of the Sabine Women." And I understood her deep embarrassment. After all, we in the west have been taught by modern museum culture that we are seeing Art, but in Beijing I could fully realize how paintings originally created to pleasure noblemen in their private chambers have been radically uprooted to be lined up in national galleries for a public trained not to see just what Li Shuyan saw.

Ever since the American sale of warplanes to Taiwan in December, the US-China relationship had been visibly strained, and this fed the foreign community's rumor mill. We heard that students who previously had been encouraged to apply for foreign study on their own were now being told that relationships with foreigners were unpatriotic. Foreign experts were being warned to avoid being too friendly with Western journalists, not to mention diplomatic staff. Now American vice president George H. W. Bush was due to arrive in Beijing in May for high-level consultations on the issue, and Friendship Hotel residents were given a briefing by senior journalists from Xinhua news agency. It sounded to me as though the official position now was that the aircraft sale was "water under the bridge." However, Xinhua representatives also said to us Americans that the Chinese authorities wanted reassurance that future relations were on a positive trajectory, or they risked being "downgraded." A visiting political scientist from Berkeley reported being publicly grilled by his academic hosts at the banquet held to welcome him at Beida. Back at the Beijing embassy, staff were scrambling to apologize privately for an article published in *Harper's* magazine by an American scholar just returned from a semester teaching at a school in the city of Zhengzhou. "China Stinks!" screamed the headline: "It May be a Nice Place to Visit but a Billion People Live There." The Yetman kids happened to be left at home while their parents took a trip for the weekend, and they took the occasion to hang from their apartment window a huge banner in their scrawled grade-school ideographs. "Long Live the USA!" it said. The Hotel's foreign experts bureau did not appreciate their progress in learning to read and write Chinese. It was quickly torn down.

Signs of tension came closer to home in late May. Lisa Wichser, an American resident of the Friendship Hotel, was arrested in the middle of the night and taken away by the police. I slept through the raid, though she lived only three entryways away from me. For several days no one among my Hotel acquaintances knew anything of this. The first accounts available to us were coming from the service staff, who obviously had been briefed. Then some residents were getting inquiries from stateside reporters pursuing the case, which had broken in the American press. Over the following couple of weeks, our "backstairs news service" struggled to understand details. Expat friends at the Hotel knew that she was a degree candidate in economics at the University of Denver, that she spoke excellent Chinese, and that she was doing research on the contemporary Chinese economy. And that she had a Chinese boyfriend who worked for the Institute for Economic Research and who was helping her.

With this as foundation, the rumor mill went into high gear. She was accused of being a CIA agent; she was "stealing state secrets"; she was "engaging in activities unauthorized by her unit." Maybe it was done by agents trying to damage US–Chinese rapprochement at a sensitive juncture (Following Bush, Howard Baker, at the time Senate majority leader, was due to visit Beijing). The American embassy was trying to keep it out of the US media; or, the American embassy had been eager for it to get maximum publicity. Then there was the intriguing issue of Lisa's Chinese boyfriend: some speculated that it had been a real romantic relationship and that they had applied to get married. Others said the romance was a cover for their scholarly collaboration. Or he was scheming to use her to get to the United States. Or he was spying on *her*.

This incident highlighted the difficulty facing many of us—foreigners doing research on politically sensitive topics, where one had to go under the table. Most meaningful economic data, which was available to central ministries for planning, was "*neibu*" or classified. I had heard about *neibu* from my students, some of whom had access to such materials when they were used for mandatory political discussion groups. An awful lot was "classified" and then actually printed in a *neibu* press. And almost everyone at the Hotel had used the "back door" for something—even a little thing like getting a Chinese colleague to borrow books for you might be twisted and used as evidence of bad intent. Forced to guess where the boundaries actually might lie, and whether to test them, foreign researchers were left suspecting that the whole Wichser affair had been set up as a warning to *us*. We too were learning to understand the well-known saying: "kill the chicken to frighten the monkeys."

Of course, the notion at the Hotel that it was all about *us* reflected the culture of paranoia that went along with the foggy informal "news service" that swirled indistinctly around us. A few weeks later I heard from an American scholar doing research in Beijing, who claimed to know from sources at Denver University that the whole affair could be traced back to factional splits in the Chinese Academy of Social Sciences. They had originally sponsored Lisa's job as a teacher in Beijing, in return for which a high cadre's daughter got a graduate student fellowship at Denver University. An Academician was in fact passing along sensitive information, and Lisa's relationship with a Chinese boyfriend from her school could draw attention to this. To allay suspicion she found a new boyfriend from outside her unit, but this did not help either her or the Academician, who was now in jail.

Was this indeed the ultimate insider story? As they accumulated layers and elisions, the various stories made less and less sense to me. They told most about us. Hotel residents who saw themselves as friends of China were inclined to blame foreign researchers for being indiscreet and getting Chinese nationals into trouble. Those who felt that their own projects were vulnerable tried to convince themselves that their work was not "sensitive." At the American embassy, diplomats wanted to believe that the Chinese Foreign Ministry was embarrassed and to blame the security police. Almost everyone was able to imagine that shadowy higher-ups were making scapegoats of

Spring Fever

minor actors. In my view the "boyfriend" who navigated the Sino–foreign contact zone would be the one in the most trouble, and about him the rumor mill was silent. We finally heard that Lisa had been deported after writing an apology, and the incident faded away.

In other contexts, however, no one seemed to care about the risks of fraternizing. Our Fulbright students had tried to arrange a bus outing to the countryside for us all, but had been told that the mountains near the Great Wall were off limits for foreigners. Sorry. Then one day a foreign expert acquaintance from the Hotel asked me if I would like join him and "some Chinese students I know," on a day trip to the country. "Just be careful," he said. "Wear a Chinese-style jacket and they will sneak us past the check points." At an assigned spot on the street near the Hotel we foreigners were picked up by a bus carrying about forty college-aged Chinese. Each of us paid two Chinese dollars (*kuai*) to the driver, and the bus was waved through the check point without stopping. After a four-hour ride we arrived at the base of an utterly wild mountain canyon carved by a stream winding through granite outcroppings and lined with thick brush and trees. One could imagine this was somewhere in California's Sierra mountains, except that above loomed the Great Wall, crumbling here, but with ancient watchtowers and warning fire towers lining the ridge leading up to the crest. Who knew where we were? Our guides were using a handwritten map someone had supplied. We did not follow the trail very far—the kids said the Great Wall itself was ten miles away—but we had a wonderful picnic.

The leader of this pied-piper band was a swashbuckling young man in his mid-twenties, who chainsmoked and did not expect to be interrupted when he talked. All the others deferred to him, and he was clearly the catch of the bunch for the young women in the group. He was good at reading their palms: short life lines, many love affairs, reversals of fortune were his stock in trade as a seer. We foreigners could not add romantic spice to the occasion, but we did facilitate conversation in English about politically incorrect topics. One fashionable young lady confided to me in a delightfully snooty sounding Chinese BBC accent how much she loved Jane Austen, and how unfair she thought it was that young people were forbidden to dance. Should she become a Christian, she asked? But she concluded, "maybe I am just a humanist." A guy who called himself "Eddie" said he had never had a real girlfriend, and wondered how once he found one and married her, they could avoid living with his parents.

These young picnickers did not belong to a common "unit" but clearly felt themselves to be part of the same social set. Nobody said, but it seemed I was getting a glimpse of the privileged children of the top leadership. Of course I learned no one's full name, and with one exception I never saw any of them again.

As we moved into June, I was ready to put aside the fraught Sino-foreign relationship and embrace the season. At the Hotel, the swimming pool was opened, and the rooftop beer garden was balmy and sociable in the evenings. Above all, my daughter Bella arrived in Beijing as soon as her high-school semester ended. This had been planned all year; she had taken a Chinese language class at UCLA extension to prepare, and she was ready for fun. Soon my Hotel apartment looked like a dorm suite, strewn with clothing, toiletries, towels, papers, and books scattered about, and I was a person with a family again. Family once again was a great solvent; my Chinese students and friends flocked to enjoy the company of a high-spirited seventeen-year-old girl with her mop of curly brown hair and her freewheeling California charm. "She is lively like a boy, not like a girl!" my students said. She went to my seminar and took over the class to answer questions about the "youth of today." "At first they asked questions about organizations and societies at school," she said. "Then they got more daring and asked about jobs and money, and then they really warmed up and asked about dancing and drugs. They almost asked me if I had a boyfriend, but shied away at the last minute."

Away from campus Li Shuyuan organized a picnic at the Summer Palace with her own high-school-aged daughter Li Chun and a school mate, both of whom got a rare afternoon off from their mothers' enforced schedule of nonstop study for college entrance exams. We all sat and ate on the famous Marble Boat, and afterwards the teenagers explored the further reaches of the park, giggling over their language malapropisms. On another day, Eddie, from the recent outing to the Great Wall, somehow appeared unannounced at the Hotel to visit— I must have mentioned my daughter's upcoming arrival to him. He was ready to take her bike riding all over town to see the sights. Fan Lanying began to help plan a trip for the three of us to the coastal resort of Beidaihe.

And the Yetmans and I, with the sullen acquiescence of Phebe, organized an end-of-semester party for the students. Michael and his wife Joan hosted at their apartment. Here there was a great deal of horseplay, a fair amount of drinking, and an incredible fuss about dancing. They all wanted to dance but nobody dared do it. Finally Michael, in a heroic display, danced with every woman in the room, including those who tried to run away, while the males gawked around the door. No Chinese man would ask any woman to dance. "Women are too dangerous," said one, only half joking. Announcing that "I am an old-fashioned woman; men have to ask me," I tried to let myself—and them—off the hook. Goaded, a pack of guys pushed Zhang Shengli forward, and the poor man stumbled through a few bars of foxtrot with me, face scarlet and hands sweating. I was touched: how did the group know that I particularly liked him?

But the semester did not end without another upheaval—a revealing comic opera that Bella and I came to call "the great exam insurrection." From the beginning of the year I had explained that my big lecture class followed American undergraduate protocols, and that these included an essay exam at the end of the semester. I had pontificated on the value of exams—forcing review and synthesis, testing critical thinking and written argument. At the end of the fall, waving aside the obvious terror of many students, I had handed out sample essay questions in advance, explaining that they would be asked to write in class on two or three of those listed. A real exam has to have grades, I said, so be prepared. Although some rumors had reached me that objections to exams had been added to the list of student grievances provoked by the case of Priscilla Oaks, the exam at the end of my fall lecture course had gone off smoothly.

At the beginning of spring semester in a Fulbright professors' meeting with Ma, it was decided that we three would each give one final exam in our respective classes. Hearing nothing further, I naïvely planned to hand out exam questions on a Wednesday in late June, ten days before the end of classes. On Tuesday evening there was a tea party with a sweet elderly Beida English professor. Ma was there but he looked distracted. Maybe, he said, I should delay handing out the questions until Friday so he could "talk to the students." I said they wanted the questions early so they would have time to study. "Phebe has decided not to give an exam," he said. Of course what Phebe did cut no ice with me; we weren't on speaking terms anyway.

What happened next made me feel like a Christian missionary who finally realizes paganism is stronger. I walked into class on Wednesday, and found an anonymous note on my desk: "We students are not willing to take the exam." When I called this a bad joke, a voice from the back of the room said, "We are willing to discuss this."

I said I would only discuss with the class monitors but my position was that if they refused to take the exam, I would refuse to teach. Bella had come with me to sit in on a lecture. "Gee, this is like high school!" she said as we two left the lecture hall.

That night Xu and the other monitors came to me. They had talked to Ma and he had told them to work it out with me. They pleaded; they tried to flatter me—I was the most conscientious of the three teachers, they said. They blamed Ma: he had promised them that there would be only one exam at the end of the spring term, but he didn't tell the teachers. Of course they as students could not say anything individually; Ma had been away and unavailable, and on his return he kept saying, "no problem." But there were many problems: he was a bad leader, he did nothing about their complaints, he cared more about pleasing the foreigners, especially Phebe. What, they asked, had happened to Priscilla Oak's Bibles? Did I know he had diverted some English language novels away from the Fulbright students and to Beida graduate students? When I turned the topic back to them as students, protesting that their last-minute classroom rebellion had been disrespectful and discourteous, they squirmed, but they would not budge. They were desperate, they were tired, maybe they were lazy. I should be practical, I was too idealistic, etc. They would only take the exam under orders and only Ma could give the order.

Of course I knew I had lost, even as I countered by asking if they liked the image of themselves as either personally irresponsible or submitting only to orders. To bring in Ma was to pass the buck for a decision that they ought to see as theirs alone. But when the individualistic Protestant ethic meets Chinese collective norms, it is likely to be no contest. Protesting their personal liking for me and their fervent desire for a pleasant ending, they left.

The last act of the comedy played out the following morning. I met with Ma and Guan in the library while the lead monitor waited outside the office door and the students waited in the classroom. Ma and Guan launched into a compliant about the students: they had been ruined morally by the evil influence of the Cultural Revolution; they had no respect; some of them were still acting like Red Guards. But in discussing the exam in front of the class monitor in the hall, Ma would only say, "it is my opinion," and "I suggest." I could tell the monitor enjoyed his discomfiture. And I felt sorry for Ma; he had been told to please several masters, and ended exposing his own powerlessness. Afterwards he and Guan admitted they had promised the students there would be only one exam (Michael Yetman's) and had not told me. Their final comment to me was that this was nothing compared to the Cultural Revolution.

Gradually the dust settled. Somewhat shamefaced, students—at least the ones who cared about my good opinion—dropped by the Hotel in ones, twos and threes. Enjoy your family, they said, take a rest, see the sights, we didn't mean to be rude. A few of them seemed to be more frank, even as they warned me not to believe what people say. Zhao Yueying recapitulated her bitter memories of how her adored father had been publicly beaten and kept under house arrest for four years. "People like you [two], who are honest and stubborn, will suffer for these qualities," she said. But she thought Ma was a bad leader, who said one thing to the students and another to the Fulbright teachers. Zhang Shengli let me know that he was studying for Michael Yetman's exam even though Michael was exempting students like him who had performed satisfactorily on the fall semester exam. "I might learn something. Even if I get a low pass, it doesn't matter." When I asked him whether students felt that exam grades could seriously hurt their careers, he explained that reports on the year would go back to their home campus work units. If grades were included in this report, anything less than an A would be risky. I explained to him that I had pushed matters partly because it was maddening to be kept in the dark because you are a foreigner: if you seem to accept everything at face value, you are considered stupid; if you question, you are being unfriendly. "Yes," he said. "We are not allowed to tell you things. It is difficult to be a foreigner here, but not as difficult as to be a Chinese."

Ma also attempted to make amends. Coming over to my apartment, accompanied by Fan, he tried to explain that cadres like himself are under discipline, and that that we Americans don't always understand the political context of all Sino-American interactions. Someone had sent an anonymous letter to the Ministry of Education complaining that Furth's classes conveyed a "bourgeois point of view" and that Ma had been too friendly with the foreign teachers in the program. The activist students took advantage of this party-line framing of the problem in the critical student meeting over the exams. Fan explicated this dynamic from her own experience: "The ringleaders are active... the ones who speak claim to represent the group, and the rest are silent. They don't like it but they can do nothing."

And, as often with tea-cup storms, larger relationships were playing a role. At the end of our meeting Ma asked me to go to the American embassy and explain to Diane Johnston, the cultural attaché, that the authorities at the Ministry of Education were forbidding him to go to the embassy and report on his recent trip to the United States. This trip, it turned out, was why he had been unavailable for several weeks earlier in the spring. The embassy had paid for an introductory tour, anticipating future collaborations between the Americans and Chinese academia. Accordingly, I trotted off to the embassy to see Diane. She was incensed at first: "He is hiding something. Maybe he got out of line in the United States and one of his travel companions was reporting on him. Everyone knows he hasn't always been straightforward, and he must know people talk." But then she softened—his position at Beida was weak, he had no academic standing, but was dependent upon a personal relationship with Vice President Huang, who used him as a troubleshooter. She ended up seeing him as vulnerable, fighting in obscure ways to rescue his career, dealing with the Faustian bargain of his job as liaison with the Americans. The truth was we both liked him.

In the end the students all got European-style final grades: "pass with honors" for a few and simple "pass" for everybody else. The final comment came from Xu Xunfeng, always adept at navigating the shoals of politics. "These days it is still safer to be Left."

Figure 8. Fan and Bella at Beidaihe beach (June 1982).

Spring Fever 121

Figure 9. Official photo of program graduates, Beijing University (June 1982).

Chapter 9

Departures

After a glorious summer of travels, at the end of August I got my wish. As Monty and Bella returned to Los Angeles, I had permission, arranged by Ma, to stay on for two months in the fall to do research; I would live at Shaoyuan, the new foreign scholars' residence on the Beida campus. A couple dozen graduate students and visiting scholars were already there. Joining the rather large English-language contingent were two incoming Fulbright professors assigned to Beida academic departments. The Chinese Fulbright program was making its transition to the normal global pattern for these exchanges.

The Shaoyuan was indeed a more comfortable, if less luxurious, accommodation for me. It offered only single rooms, with a toilet and shower down the hall, and a simple cafeteria for meals. But students and other Chinese visitors could come and go freely, as an elderly porter/watchman waved them past the entrance without signing in. Moreover, I had left behind the alienated global drifters who had so often dominated table talk at the Friendship Hotel. My new colleagues included China specialists I knew from back home, and most of the others also wanted to study, teach, or do research in Beijing.

My own research went well. I had settled on a project of studying women in the literature of classical Chinese medicine, where my interest in traditional knowledge that was valued in the PRC offset a potentially unsettling feminist agenda. However, compared to teaching, research was a mole's work, burrowing in libraries and struggling all day with books and translations. It offered few opportunities to make new Chinese friends. I relied on Fan and Li, and soon was very glad I would be home by Thanksgiving. But these two months did give me a deeper look into the strategies involved in "scheming to go abroad."

From the moment I arrived at the Friendship Hotel the previous September, I had been repeatedly approached by Chinese looking to travel to the United States. All sorts of people—daughters of an acquaintance who was a visiting professor at UCLA, Chinese colleagues of other foreign experts—wanted help with application forms, introductions to Southern California academics, advice for their children graduating from high school, and more. Whatever their motives—curiosity, ambition, cabin fever—I soon learned to turn these appeals aside. My own students were more discreet, especially because Sino-American relations had soured sometime in the fall of 1981. Xu Xunfeng later explained privately to me that the government stopped encouraging people to apply on their own to study abroad, and that the Fulbright students were being sternly exhorted to avoid exploiting their relation with us American professors to find sponsors. Only one student approached me privately, and because he was not one I knew well, it was easy to gently discourage him.

Li Shuyan had been one of those who had responded to the earlier directives encouraging people to apply on their own to study abroad.

As a mid-career academic in good standing, she could reasonably hope to be accepted for a fellowship at the University of Toronto. But as spring advanced, she had fretted to me that "the government is making all sorts of trouble for me." In the end, in spite of the fact that Toronto was willing to receive her, the authorities at her home university told her she had to wait. Others in her unit had priority and that was that.

Mulling over her situation that autumn, Li mused that it seemed to her strange that before liberation Chinese who studied abroad returned home freely, but now the dream was that those who left for America would find happiness there. It would be interesting to write a work of fiction about these "cultural frontiers," she said. She had worked out a plot: a woman lost contact with her father thirty years ago, and he is now abroad and rich. Angry with the father who has deserted her, this woman does not let her daughter go abroad. But when the mother dies, the daughter makes the trip and finds her grandfather, who helps support her as she makes a new life. I later realized this story line was a thinly veiled reflection on Shuyan's own life story of the father who had gone off to Taiwan in 1949, leaving her and her mother behind. Here the dream of going abroad seemed to me to be entangled with a longing for family reunification that could not be fulfilled due to the scars both personal and political that divided the PRC and Taiwan. Thwarted in her own ambition, Li Shuyan began to plan for her elder daughter. No long-lost parent or grandparent appeared, but she managed to reconnect with some old friends who had emigrated to the United States in the 1950s. By the time I left China in November 1982, Li Chun was enrolled as a chemistry major at Amoy University, while her mother was working on her application to a small American college in the Midwest with missionary connections and a tradition of scholarships for students from Asia.

These last months also added more layers to my understanding of Ma Shiyi's complex life and the role of the Fulbright program in it. He of course had smoothed my way to move onto campus, and now I got to know him better. I visited his home in an apartment near campus, where he showed me a fourteenth-century Confucian primer hand-copied in elegant calligraphy: this was the text his father had prepared for Ma's early childhood education. I learned of his love for the great eighteenth century romantic novel, *Dream of the Red Chamber* (*Hongloumeng*) and for Shen Fu's touching nineteenth-century memoir about married love, *Six Chapters from a Life Adrift* (*Fousheng liuji*). He helped me gain access to the collection of medical history rare books (*shanben*) at the Academy for Traditional Chinese Medicine across town, overcoming the suspicion of its librarians that any foreign reader must be looking for secret herbal formulas that could be sold to Japanese pharmaceutical companies. And, it turned out, his wife was a trained acupuncturist, who was available to instruct me in the technical side of medical Chinese language and herbology.

Old Guan at the library told me about Ma's early career as a student activist, when he neglected his studies to devote himself to revolutionary organizing and land reform campaigns. This was often dangerous work and his father disapproved, but it catapulted Ma into a Communist Party leadership role at the reorganized Beijing University in the 1950s. But, of course, Old Guan explained, "Eighty percent of our old friends were rightists." In the early years Ma's recommendation had been enough to save Guan's job and those of others. Then in May of 1966 the Maoist leadership called on students to "storm the headquarters," and schools in Beijing became laboratories for the Red Guard movement, with calamitous consequences. I knew that as a prestigious campus close to the center of power, Beida had experienced particularly vicious and toxic fighting between Red Guard student factions, and faculty scapegoats were the victims of struggle sessions, forced labor, and physical abuse. Now I heard how in 1967 and 1968, as the tumult ruined many of his peers and the campus was a shambles, Ma spent months in one of the notorious "cowsheds"—makeshift prisons that confined "rightists," now labeled "black elements." Nonetheless, Guan said, he encouraged them all, predicting that the chaos would end: "One day, you will see, they will come to us begging us to go back to work." Guan's eulogy evoked an image of touching loyalty among survivors of Beida's trauma during the Cultural Revolution, and of the grit it took to try and work together for the university's renewal afterwards.

Now I was also getting to know Ma's wife, Zhang Jingli. Pretty and petite, she also was part of this intertwined community of Beida old-timers, for she had graduated from the exclusive girls' high school where Guan's father had long ago been the principal. Marriage to a young Beida scholar who had abandoned German philosophy for revolution would have been advantageous for a girl with a suspect class background in the 1950s. But it turned out to cost her dearly. In the Cultural Revolution, their two younger children had died, she said, when they fell ill and were turned away from the hospital: "black elements" were refused care, and in any case all the good doctors had been sent out of the capital to serve peasants in the countryside. One son, now about thirteen years old, survived.

It was Fan who explained to me the dilemma surrounding this boy, who had the English name Thomas, but who everyone called "the young monkey king." He was attending a Beida neighborhood junior high school even though he did not qualify by examination. Apparently the school had enrolled a whole class of similar low achievers, whose parents all worried that their youngsters would become delinquents. Somehow—its exact origin remained vague—the idea percolated that Thomas might get abroad to a good high school in the United States. Fan thought that a returned professor from the 1980–1981 Fulbright year wanted to sponsor the boy, but his loose talk about these plans in Washington, DC, only compromised Ma back in China, leaving him doubly vulnerable, torn between his socialist and family obligations.

No one approached me about young Thomas Ma's future, for it turned out that they had other hopes. But Zhang Jingli was fed up. Maybe the marriage was on the rocks as well; I never asked. She wanted to leave China. She had met the director of a Chinese medicine clinic in California who was ready to hire her. But of course her work unit, a research academy of traditional Chinese medicine, would not give her permission. She and Ma asked if Monty and I would sponsor her visit as a tourist, which would deflect her superiors' suspicion of her plans. She would explain she needed to visit her aged, impoverished mother in Los Angeles. (This was not the first time I was surprised by the news that my Chinese associates had connections abroad.)

In this way I became Zhang Jingli's ticket to a job as an acupuncturist in Santa Barbara. Was I being manipulated? Of course, but I had learned from the year that relationships in China involve exchange of obligations, and you just have to decide if you want to trust the other parties to the exchange. We Fulbright professors had not facilitated foreign study for our students, but our Beida supervisor had covertly risked his career to enlist our aid for his own family. And we went along. I have never regretted this.

By the time I left for home in November 1982, Zhang Jingli's travel to Los Angeles was arranged. Ma's son Thomas, "the young monkey king," was to be enrolled in a New England boarding school arranged by Phebe Chao, and Fan Lanying was studying for the TOEFL test in hopes that one of her Fulbright professors from the 1980–1981 year would offer sponsorship.

As for Ma, I am sure he never wanted to leave China. Still committed to socialism, he remained a hopeful man. The last time I saw him was when he passed through Los Angeles in 1983. He had been promoted to be deputy director of the Beida library and charged with buying Western-language books for Beida and twenty-seven other major Chinese universities. It was a prestigious assignment: the World Bank had given one hundred million dollars for the project, which was supervised directly by the State Council, insulated from regular academic and educational bureaucracies. Besides Ma, another academic leader of the project was Xie Xide, a senior biochemist from Fudan University in Shanghai. Explaining his mission to us in Los Angeles, Ma was graceful and conscientious about this responsibility. Concerned that the book lists generated by his Beida academic colleagues would be sadly out of date, he was searching around for guidance from library science professionals. We knew we were unable to help him much but wished him well.

Then in 1986 we learned he had come to the United States one last time—to die. Though only in his early fifties, he had been diagnosed with stomach cancer—a common malady among Chinese men in his generation. A wealthy New Yorker involved in Sino-American business exchanges—who remained anonymous—paid for a last-ditch trip to Sloane Kettering in Manhattan for treatment. Ma's wife and his son Thomas were there with him at the end. Fan Lanying, by then an ESL graduate student in upstate New York, was there too. None of the three of them ever returned home to China.

Epilogue

As I think back on this narrative after thirty-five years, a long view seems called for. After all I am a historian writing about a place that I have spent my career studying, and in whose fortunes I became entangled for a time. A great tide made China's twentieth-century revolution central both to the Chinese people and to us Western outsiders whose discovery of China's history occurred during those same decades. All who rode the tide were beached in the backwash of the failures that littered the shore after Mao's death. As privileged outsiders, we Americans were the fascinated, often baffled and even horrified spectators of a socio-political upheaval that we struggled to understand. But on the other hand both actors and observers—the Chinese people and American "China hands"—shared a stage where China's revolution has been part of a global phenomenon. It resonated with dreams of an egalitarian society, of political freedom and of national liberation as old as the Enlightenment and as new as the student movements of the 1960s or the Arab Spring of 2011.

In hindsight the experimental phase of Sino-American normalization stretched from Carter's full diplomatic recognition of the PRC in January 1979 to August 1983, when the "third communiqué" between the two nations was signed, signaling the grudging Chinese acceptance of the Reagan administration's continuing commitment to the *de facto* independence of Taiwan. Then, as economic openings to foreign investment and capitalist development accelerated through the 1980s, there was rising excitement about China's liberalization until the Tiananmen massacre in 1989 cut such Western hopes short. Today I can see that my Fulbright year coincided with months of contentious negotiation over American arms sales to Taiwan—where failure would threaten to shut down cultural exchange altogether. At Beida neither we Westerners nor our Chinese students knew details of ongoing high level discussions surrounding drafts of the "third communiqué," but were constantly reminded that official suspicion and public fear still surrounded the Sino-American relationship.

When I read over the published accounts of the American journalists and diplomats who were posted to Beijing in these three years, I recognize a distinctive political atmosphere that combined hope and frustration. Diplomat Nicholas Platt would later write in *China Boys* (published in 2009) about the excitement of the 1970s and early 1980s when backstage negotiations between high-level foreign affairs professionals focused on the nuts-and-bolts of official travelling delegations, of diplomatic transition from liaison office to fully staffed embassy, and of surprisingly friendly military cooperation that lasted all the way down to 1989 and the subsequent collapse of the Soviet Union. The first mainstream American journalists with China assignments were Jay and Linda Matthews, arriving in 1979 for the *Washington Post*, and Fox Butterfield, arriving in 1980 for the *New York Times*. Confined to living and working quarters in the venerable Beijing Hotel downtown, they described an environment close to the one I experienced. They dealt with segregated living arrangements, official minders in their entourage, bureaucratic obfuscation, the shock of the monochrome cityscape, the challenge of making human contact, and the ethical dilemmas of relationships with Chinese who were keenly aware that both opportunity and danger would be involved. In *Alive in the Bitter Sea* (published in 1982), Butterfield used his reportage to provide a harsh overview of the Maoist era, describing a people he saw as disillusioned and cynical. In *One Billion: A China Chronicle* (published in 1983), the temperamentally sunnier

Epilogue

Jay and Linda Matthews were more impressed with the family and "community spirit" (their translation of *guanxi*) that had helped people cope with adversity and sometimes express optimism about the future. In spite of the fact that the American community in Beijing was tiny, diplomats, journalists, and the few resident academics like myself inhabited separate spheres and interacted with different communities of local Chinese. An expat society, with its social circles, public events, schools for children and clubs for recreation, scarcely existed. However, what we pioneers of normalization all shared was a sense that the PRC was still an impoverished and isolated country, and that the challenges of development ahead were staggering.

When a revolution is over—and it was clear that Mao's revolution was indeed over—definitions of "normal" themselves must change. Looking back historically, I can see that we Western intellectuals had been here centuries before. The reaction against republican revolution inside France in the 1790s was named "Thermidor." Over a generation it produced the individualistic Romantic movement in English and German culture, and led to a French infatuation with Napoleon. In the mid-twentieth century, as the Russian Revolution of 1917 slid gradually into Stalinist dictatorship, former sympathizers abandoned socialism and identified themselves more or less enthusiastically with the capitalist "free world" of the Cold War era. Public fascination with Maoism as part of the "third world" revolutions of the mid-twentieth century waned as the afterglow of Enlightenment ideology faded, and as decolonization created new nations just as capitalist globalization was beginning to render their borders—national, social, ethnic, religious—increasingly porous.

Over the course of the 1980s, my generation of American China scholars—only a footnote in this large picture—regrouped in many ways. Some dropped out of the academy; others reversed direction from being PRC cheerleaders to acting as liberal critics of Chinese communist authoritarianism. As someone who has been a historian first of all, I opted for the self-criticism that blamed not only political naiveté but also collective scholarly ignorance, which my year as a Fulbright had made only more visible. Normalization meant that the huge long-term history of China that I had only dimly intuited in the 1960s was opening up for modern study. All sorts of mainland sources for social, economic and cultural research were becoming available and both Chinese and foreign scholars could access them. Among American China specialists, Qing-dynasty studies began to be popular, as did global comparative history and "silk road" studies. There were flourishing investigations into law, population, environment, archeology, religion, and my own new field—gender studies as reflected in the history of Chinese medicine. My choice here could be seen as strategic. PRC scholars wanted to have the history of their pre-modern science, technology and medicine globally recognized and were willing collaborators in the project, while my own personal revolution was the feminist one. Beginning in the 1980s American academics flocked to historical study of gender and sexuality, and women China experts were part of this. Works like *Engendering China*, edited by Christina Gilmartin, Gail Hershatter, and others (Harvard University Press 1994) took feminist scholarship into the mainstream of Asian Studies. In sum, for scholars like me the aftermath of the Mao revolution was a soft landing.

Of course as it turned out post-Mao China astonished everybody. The economic transformation launched under Deng Xiaoping has made China the factory floor of the world and a global power. Beginning in the 1990s middle-class prosperity reached millions, allowing for material comforts that it would have been hard even to dream of in 1982. These include access to modern health care and to consumer goods extending to ownership of a home and perhaps a car; and it allows for personal freedom—an open, competitive job market, opportunity for travel, leisure, and entertainment. Studying and living abroad remain attractive but are no longer an overwhelming personal ambition.

Recently Wang Hui, an influential and cosmopolitan Chinese intellectual, has tried to summarize how Chinese intellectuals have thought about this new post-Mao "rising China." The English translation of his collection of essays, first written largely in the 1990s for the leading intellectual journal, *Dushu,* is titled *The End of the Revolution* (published 2009). It argues that Chinese can no longer look to Maoist ideology of class struggle and the mass line, nor can China situate itself internationally in the bipolar global system of the now defunct Cold War. In forging a path forward that is not simply an embrace of market capitalism and consumerism, he invites today's Chinese to recover an understanding of their deeper history and philosophical traditions that the revolutions of the twentieth century effaced. His own work on traditional society in fact emphasizes philosophical currents since the sixteenth century that resonate with Enlightenment aspirations for science, rationality, and modern citizenship. Wang also suggests that for all its excesses, the Maoist revolution will be remembered and honored for forging a modern sovereign nation, and for giving the common people a language with which to call for social justice and fight corruption and inequality. He does not use the words "freedom" or "human rights." Here he conforms to official discourse that remains suspicious of Western intentions, much as our own mainstream narratives continue to make the Cultural Revolution and the Tiananmen massacre touchstones for understanding contemporary China as a Communist Party dictatorship.

I have not kept up with most of my former students who stayed in the PRC, scattered back to many home provinces after the Fulbright year ended. But I would like to think they have shared in the prosperity of the last twenty-five years and that some of them have even flourished inside and outside the academy. They will have had freedom to divorce, and because most spent their reproductive years under the one-child policy, they are unlikely to have had many children. Given the importance of kinship networks in so many of their stories of life growing up in the Maoist era, I wonder whether they remain satisfied with the shrunken nuclear family that is becoming standard today. And I wonder how my former women students have responded, as invitations to embrace sexualized youthful lifestyles have overshadowed an official state-sponsored policy of "women hold up half the sky." As for the aspirations for democracy that underlay my teaching, my sense is that American electoral politics, already suspect then, have not gained luster with many inside the PRC since. (Indeed, in 2016 some of their critiques seem eerily prescient.) But I imagine that many want to see criminal justice reform, environmental protection, and a crackdown on abuses of power in China's far-flung bureaucracies. The implied social contract of Deng Xiaoping and his successors has been for leadership to offer economic progress and a measure of personal autonomy in exchange for ceding political power to the Party. In this updated version of a very old "mandate of Heaven," the public looks to the state for solutions to problems. This implied contract has so far held, but its future stability cannot be guaranteed. All modern societies struggle between equalitarian and meritocratic models of social justice; all deal with unearned privilege and abuse of power. I remain a friend of China, hoping for dialogue that highlights problems that we share in an increasingly crowded and interconnected planet.

Praise for the Book

"Charlotte Furth's memoir provides a window into a China that few of us can remember or even believe possible: a country that was not the economic and political powerhouse of today, but a hesitant, slightly paranoid society emerging from decades of being closed-off to the outside world. As one of the rare witnesses to this crucial transition, Professor Furth takes us into the life of China's most important university, showing the struggle to accept her group of visiting scholars—a microcosm for the debate in China at the time over whether the country really should open up. Written honestly and candidly, this memoir will be of interest to scholars of US-China engagement but also to general readers eager to see how much China has changed over the past decades."

—Ian Johnson,
Beijing correspondent for *The New York Times*, and author of *The Souls of China: The Return of Religion After Mao*

* * * * *

"Charlotte Furth, a distinguished scholar of China's past, turns her gaze now on a special moment of her own. The resulting memoir is alternately amusing and moving. Written in an engaging and candid style, this book is a pleasure to read and opens a fascinating window on an intriguing but little studied moment in recent Chinese history."

—Jeffrey Wasserstrom,
editor of *The Oxford Illustrated History of Modern China*

* * * * *

"The scale and reach of China's transformation since the death of Mao challenges historical perspective. Few Americans today have any sense of how far China has come since it's opening in the early 1980s. Charlotte Furth was there to see the start of the defrost with the country's opening and her lively account of her experiences in China then provides a unique and invaluable record. Hers is a touching, gentle, humorous, and thoughtful story. It is also useful in these days of rising tensions between China and the United States to be reminded of China's social reality not very long ago."

—Gordon H. Chang,
Olive H. Palmer Professor in Humanities,
Stanford University
and author of *Fateful Ties:
A History of America's Preoccupation with China*

* * * * *

"Written in a sober, yet intimate, tone, Charlotte Furth's memoir of her time teaching in China during the very early years of the reform era brings to life the tensions, contradictions, and promises of that period. A famed historian writing about her personal experience, Furth gives us a vivid portrayal of a China 'on the verge,' and of the emotions, fears, and hopes it elicited in those who saw it up close. This book is a gem for specialists and curious onlookers alike."

—Fabio Lanza,
Department of History, University of Arizona

Praise for the Book

* * * * *

"As a trained China historian and astute observer, Charlotte Furth has provided us with a nuanced and well-crafted narrative of her life as a foreign teacher at a major Chinese university emerging from the trauma of the Cultural Revolution. As one of the first Fulbright teachers in China after 1949, she was sailing in uncharted waters, but managed to impart a better understanding of the United States for her students, while gaining their trust. She has perfectly captured the ambiance and environment of Beijing in the early 1980's: poverty, the winter stockpiles of cabbage, the hordes of cyclists, dust storms, lack of personal choice, bureaucratic restrictions, and 'spiritual pollution.' From the encounters she describes, the reader will appreciate the continuing importance of social relationships while working and living in China, especially in successfully coping with the madding ambiguity of Chinese bureaucracy and opaque social norms."

—John Thomson,
first Counselor for Press and Cultural Affairs,
American Embassy in Beijing (1979–1981)

* * * * *

"In this engaging memoir of the early days of China's opening to the outside world, Charlotte Furth captures the strangeness of a time when few foreigners lived in Beijing and no Chinese could be sure which way was forward—or whether that way could include knowing people like her. As she recalls the affection and puzzlement she felt responding to their hopes and fears, she is able to show us the contradictions and disappointments with which that generation, stranded between Maoism and modernity, had to cope. China's opening may not have been easy for the foreigners who went to live there, but as one of her students told her, 'It is difficult to be a foreigner here, but not as difficult as to be a Chinese.' Furth fills this gap with a thoughtful compassion that we would do well to nurture still."

—Timothy Brook,
author of *Vermeer's Hat* and *Mr. Selden's Map of China*

* * * * *

About the Author

Charlotte Furth is Professor Emerita of Chinese History at the University of Southern California. Before moving to USC in 1989, she spent two decades on the faculty of California State University at Long Beach. The book based on her Stanford PhD dissertation, *Ting Wen-chiang: Science and China's New Culture*, was published by Harvard East Asian Monograph Series in 1970. *A Flourishing Yin: Gender in China's Medical History* (University of California Press, 1999) was awarded the "Women in Science" prize by the History of Science Society in 2001. For her scholarship and service to the profession, including work as journal editor and on several important edited volumes, she was honored for "Distinguished Contributions to Asian Studies" by the Association for Asian Studies in 2012. She lives in Los Angeles.

Figure 10. Photo of the author (2017).

www.ingramcontent.com/pod-product-compliance
Lightning Source LLC
Chambersburg PA
CBHW031458160426
43195CB00010BB/1022